Isaiah Speaks

Isaiah Speaks

A Voice from the Past for the Present

Merrill Morse

RESOURCE *Publications* • Eugene, Oregon

ISAIAH SPEAKS
A Voice from the Past for the Present

Wipf & Stock
An Imprint of Wipf and Stock Publishers
199 W. 8th Ave., Suite 3
Eugene, OR 97401
www.wipfandstock.com

ISBN 13: 978-1-62032-157-7
Manufactured in the U.S.A.

Contents

Preface

THERE ARE PERHAPS THREE Isaiahs. So scholars say. The first was a real person whose name got assigned to a whole collection of prophetic writings in the Old Testament. But the writings in this collection come from multiple sources. How do we know that? The writings themselves reveal it.

The first thirty-nine chapters or so of the book called Isaiah stem from the prophetic ministry of a recognizable individual whose term of service is described explicitly in the very first verses of his testimony:

> The vision of Isaiah the son of Amoz,
> which he saw concerning Judah and Jerusalem
> in the days of Uzziah, Jotham, Ahaz, and Hezekiah, kings of Judah.
> Isaiah 1:1 (RSV)

We know when Abraham Lincoln lived (1809–1865), and we can look up who was president before and after him. The same holds true for the kings mentioned in Isaiah. Though the time period we are considering with Isaiah (two thousand seven hundred years ago) is a bit fuzzy in terms of precise dates, for example, whether Ahaz became king in 735 or in 731 BCE, we can reasonably identify ballpark dates for people and events of that time.

There are "extra-biblical" records to go by, too: government documents, military records, and miscellaneous references to current events of those times that help us put the biblical account in context. The Assyrians, for example, who were the dominant power in Isaiah's day, kept records which referred to some of the very people and places mentioned in Isaiah's writings (you can still see their impressive carved depictions of the siege of Lachish in 701 BCE in the British Museum in London). Later, the Babylonians and Persians who replaced the Assyrians as the world powers of their day, created records of their own, reporting, for example, the captivity and release of the Jews who were taken into Exile to Babylon.

Together with the biblical record itself, it is easy to see that some parts of the book called Isaiah were probably written more than a hundred years after the stories of Uzziah, Hezekiah, and the like were recorded. Isaiah was no Methuselah and no one has claimed him to be, so obviously, unless Isaiah's prophetic gift was one that allowed him—Nostradamus-like—to peer centuries into the future (which some Christians do believe), someone else authored the majestic and inspiring prophecies and the historical passages of the latter half of the biblical book, such as the reference to the Persian king, Cyrus (600?–529 BCE) in chapter 45 of Isaiah.

The later chapters are wedded to First Isaiah for a reason, however. Prophets in those days had disciples, followers, and students, just as did the great Greek philosophers, or renowned teachers today. "Prophetic schools" preserved the traditions and themes associated with their leaders, though, of course, these schools morphed over time as new insights were developed and added. The fact that sixty-six chapters from multiple sources are woven together in the body of work called Isaiah is a reflection of the sense of biblical editors—those who assembled the Old Testament as we know it today—who saw these materials as linked by style, subject, theme, and the like.

Scholars will forever debate the fine points of who or what group wrote this passage or that and for what purpose and when and in what context. That is their job. For the purpose of this book, it is enough to know that the portions of Isaiah presented here are generally seen as belonging to the life and work of a brilliant, insightful, devout, and passionate man who looked at the world around him, wrote about it in dramatic terms, and did his best to tell it what God led him to.

People today are doing the same thing. Some of those have influenced the creation and character of this book and need to be acknowledged. Chief among them is Kosuke Koyama, whose imagination and deeply insightful theological writing has demonstrated what is possible in the global community when it comes to relating faith and culture in an inter-religious context. Lesslie Newbigin, Walter Hollenweger, and William Smalley were also inspiring role models in passionately and articulately pursuing the conversation between faith and culture in a global context. To these particular mentors as well as to the less-renowned but equally sustaining members of the numerous communities of faith which have so enriched one's life over the years, from Japan to England to Minnesota, I owe a deep debt in heart, mind, and soul. To them be thanks, and to God, glory.

Merrill Morse

1

Introduction

"The vision which Isaiah, son of Amoz,
had concerning Judah and Jerusalem . . ."

ISAIAH 1:1A (NAB)

WHAT DOES IT MEAN to have a vision? Politicians try to convince voters during election campaigns that they are people of vision. Like a latter-day Moses, the politician says, "Follow me, and I will lead you to a promised land of security and economic prosperity." Business and religious organizations are constantly creating vision statements. The very process of doing so is supposed to help discern direction, unite members, and motivate employees, congregants, stakeholders, donors, and the like. Vision language is meant to inspire trust and hope, to garner loyalty and support.

Is that what Isaiah was doing? Was he trying to attract customers, win the confidence of his followers, or establish public credibility? When the editors of the book of Isaiah chose "vision language" to begin their story about this extraordinary prophet and the God whose word Isaiah proclaimed, was it to get the attention of potential religious "voters"? Was it part of a campaign to convince people to cast their lot with the particular religious school of thought represented by these prophetic writings? Of course it was!

But it was also a great deal more. To be a prophet touched by God in the Hebrew world of the eighth century BCE was no ordinary experience. To be caught up in a *bona fide* vision of biblical dimensions was not only a religious experience but also a social, psychological, political, and even physical event. The prophets of Isaiah's age were unlike any group around today. As members of a special class within the religious, social, and political culture of their day, a prophet's vision could embarrass family members, alienate friends, offend people in power, and change world history.

But once touched by God, what choice did a prophet have? What choice would any of us have, given a comparable experience? A prophet's words could intimidate kings, enrage the rich, and frighten just about everybody. The strange acts which sometimes accompanied their prophetic witness (such as walking around naked for three years, as Isaiah had done in obedience to God's instructions—Isaiah 20:2–3), could make them the laughing stock of the whole community and even endanger their lives.

As one commentator (J. Muilenburg in *Peake's Commentary on the Bible*) has put it, "The prophets of Israel were aware that the unseen world had impinged upon their consciousness." The question is, has it impinged on ours? Is reading Isaiah merely an academic exercise? Or does God have something to say today via these ancient texts? Can Isaiah's vision be ours or can we share in the prophetic experience for the world of our day? Such questions—perhaps as an invitation—are what this book is about.

First, we will delve into the words and world of Isaiah. Then, we will try to relate it to our own lives and the world in which we daily live. Reading alone does not suffice to address such questions. Reflection and prayer can enrich the experience, especially if shared with others. Accordingly, space for reflection will be included with the written journey, as well as questions to ponder and discuss, along with prayers to stimulate a response to the texts. The texts themselves, it should be noted, are excerpts from the relevant chapters of Isaiah. The reader may find it interesting to peruse verses or passages that are not included in these essays by reading with a Bible at hand. Various versions will do, since various translations are already utilized in this book. Along the way, we will seek to get in touch with a fascinating man from antiquity who lived much as we do, wrestling with the questions of turbulent times.

For Discussion

1. Of all the people you know or have met, who would you consider a prophet and why?
2. Would you say you have a spiritual vision towards life, and if so, what would you identify as the primary shaping factors for your vision (e.g., family, religious community, culture, education)?

For Reflection

Craft a "vision statement" for your life. Identify the driving beliefs and values that you would like to guide your existence and your interactions with others. Factor in whether and how "the unseen world has impinged upon your consciousness." Consider the impact your vision is having on others and on the world around you.

For Prayer

Vision-giving God, open our eyes, open our hearts. Prepare us daily to receive the revelations around us so that we may discern your redeeming presence. Impinge upon our consciousness, we pray, that we may live with inspiration, assurance, and direction. Amen.

2

Jerusalem

"The vision of Isaiah the son of Amoz,
which he saw concerning Judah and Jerusalem . . ."

ISAIAH 1:1A (RSV)

YEARS AGO I SAT leaning back against a tree on a bare patch of dirt just outside the walls of the Old City of Jerusalem. In my worn canvas duffle bag were a couple of boiled eggs, some chunks of bread, and a cat-food-sized tin of some kind of fish that actually tasted pretty good. The free lunch came compliments of the agricultural kibbutz where I worked as a volunteer. I still remember the dusty blue blazer I wore and the pair of pants with a slight split in the crotch which I only noticed later, and which probably accounted for the bemused smile on the face of a man who wished me *b'teh avon*—the Hebrew equivalent of *bon appétit*—as he walked by on the street.

For that fragment of time, sitting under the tree in the shadow of the Old City, I was not just a tourist, a passing visitor through the holy city of Jerusalem. Instead I was part of the fabric of its ordinary life—split pants and all—a living molecule in an organism over three thousand years old. That's the magic. That's the mystery of Jerusalem and of the rolling hills surrounding it, the whole region of Judah. It isn't just land. It's a story.

The book of Isaiah provides a piece of the story, about how a man from Jerusalem had a vision concerning this dusty speck of the planet's surface. That vision totally reordered his life, compelling him to spend it cajoling, threatening, pleading, promising, and otherwise engaging the people who lived there. Ultimately, his vision became immortalized as a text not only for the people who first experienced it, but for believers everywhere in the centuries that followed.

What was the shape of this vision? Did Isaiah's vision concerning Judah and Jerusalem come as a series of dreams or visions in his head, as we commonly imagine for prophets? Perhaps not. Perhaps some of Isaiah's prophecy simply came from his everyday experience and expertise being molded by God into a divine message. After all, Isaiah was probably a member of "high society" in Jerusalem. The court language he employs and the conversations he records indicate that he had access to kings and people in power. Perhaps some of the insights and messages in his vision reflected conclusions he had drawn from his time spent in the royal court. Isaiah was an educated man, as capable of political, religious, and social reflection as anyone today. Could part of his vision have included not only direct revelation but also informed common sense? And couldn't this be divinely inspired by a God who gives us brains and a conscience to use for making responsible decisions and moral judgments for the world in which we live?

But who is to say what makes a vision divinely inspired? How do we know if a vision comes from God? The biblical and historical criteria generally revolve around: (a) whether the message is consistent with the larger biblical record of God's words and deeds in the life of the people, and (b) whether or not the way history unfolds validates the prophet's message. Isaiah's vision passes the test on both counts.

What about our visions today? How do we know who is speaking for God in our time? Of course, history will tell, as it did for the prophets. But in the meantime, there is the consistency criterion. How does the message accord with the wisdom of the family of faith worldwide?

Trouble is, the Bible can be used to support almost any position we want it to, for example, to support slavery, apartheid, the subservience of women (as it has been in the past), or to support a host of political and theological positions in today's world. Our only real hope for certainty, short of time travel, is to test contemporary prophetic voices against the views and experiences of the faith community as a whole. Individual sects or even denominations can proclaim all kinds of visions and social conclusions in the name of God. But how do these visions stand up to a dialogue with the whole, historical, global community of believers? Certainly, divine inspiration is much too important and complex to be subject to majority vote. And the human community of faith is far too diverse—even within particular faith traditions—to yield universal agreement on God's presence and actions. But by holding our visions up for the broader scrutiny of fellow believers, we may at least stand a better chance of making them more than self-serving.

Isaiah faced a similar test. While he was proclaiming gloom and doom, making a lot of people uncomfortable, there were no doubt prophets with perspectives different from his own who were blessing the status quo, calling Isaiah a quack, and reassuring the rich, powerful, and apostate that all would be well. We don't know a lot about Isaiah's opponents because they were consigned to the dust bin of history. That Isaiah is still with us, however, testifies to the enduring merit of his message.

A fearful set of questions remains for us, however: "What is God saying today? Who speaks for God? How do we know?"

For Discussion

1. On what basis do you determine who speaks for God?
2. Do you automatically trust your pastor, rabbi, imam? Should you?

For Reflection

Find a picture of Jerusalem from your bible, a book, the internet or wherever—preferably one of those grand panoramic, bird's-eye-view vistas of the city. Now imagine yourself in the picture somewhere, perhaps standing by a tree in the courtyard of the grand gold-domed shrine where Abraham is said to have laid Isaac to be sacrificed. Or, envision placing your hand on one of the huge limestone blocks of the walls around the Old City. Picture the hands of the pilgrims before you, touching the same wall. Envision them passing by on foot or donkey or even peering out from the endless flow of tourist buses visiting this ancient abode of prophets, peasants, and kings. Recall the Roman soldiers and invading armies who passed through this region. Feel the history. You can bond with this city, a city that lives so vividly in the psyche of at least half of the earth's population.

Now pray. Like Pope John Paul II inserting a prayer for peace into the space between the great blocks of the Western Wall, insert a prayer into the holy space of your day (write it down, if you'd like). Claim your presence in the cosmic story along with the place held by those around you, especially those closest to you. Remember Isaiah and the people of Jerusalem and Judah who lived the story before us and from whose lives we are learning. Trust that God will provide the kind of vision needed for our world today as it was provided via Isaiah to our forbears in faith.

For Prayer

Vision-giving God, open our minds to see what Isaiah saw, so that we may perceive your involvement in our world today. Teach us to listen for your guidance, to heed your words of warning, to discern what is most essential for faithful living amidst the many competing claims for our spiritual loyalty. Thank you for including us, for inviting us into this incredible story. Amen.

3

Identity

"The vision of Isaiah the son of Amoz, which he saw . . .
in the days of Uzziah, Jotham, Ahaz, and Hezekiah, kings of Judah"

ISAIAH 1:1 (RSV)

I LIKE TO TELL people that I was arrested by the CIA. But that is not true. What actually happened was that the local US AID officer in Luang Prabang thought we were hippies looking for drugs. That is why his assistant pulled up beside us in an unpaved alley and offered us a ride in his open-roofed jeep. But when we climbed in, he actually drove us to a small US government compound to be examined by his supervisor, who, it was widely believed, worked for the CIA.

To back up a bit . . . this was Laos, 1968. The Viet Nam war was in full swing. Luang Prabang, once the royal capital of the Kingdom of Laos, was located in the central mountains about an hour's flight north of the modern-day capital, Vientiane. Overland travel or river travel along the Mekong River to Luang Prabang was considered dangerous, though some travelers dared it.

As naïve college students on Thanksgiving break from a study-abroad program in Bangkok, Thailand, three of us had paid ten dollars each for a flight to the small ancient city. Besides adventure, our goal was to see the ornate gold-covered *bas relief* walls of the beautiful temple and palace buildings of past Lao kings which sat atop a hill wrapped on two sides by a bend in the Mekong River.

Traveling cheap, we slept on the floor of a lantern storage room in the basement of a Buddhist temple. As if it were not spooky enough curling up by candle light on the blanket-less straw mats in the low space under the eerie red lanterns, the night was made more dramatic by the wooden window shutters being periodically jerked open to reveal clusters of young, saffron-robed monks peering in to observe what three white strangers (two male, one female) might be up to.

It was the next day that we were delivered to the man we suspected was CIA. He stood before us in a plain, grey office room in front of a desk, a chair, and a few metal filing cabinets. Looking us over with an icy glare, he demanded our passports. Without words he meticulously examined the first, then the second, snapping each one shut with the flair of a German train conductor. Finally, he stared at mine in extended silence before muttering the words, "I'll be damned!" The three of us, already nervous, glanced at each other with increasing anxiety. But what came next was another "I'll be damned!" and then a third, louder "Well, I'll be damned." Finally, he looked up and said, "You're Mart Morse's son, aren't you? I used to shop in his grocery store. I grew up near Trent, South Dakota, just up the road." There in the mountains of central Laos, on the edge of a war, halfway around the world from home, I was identified by my lineage.

Isaiah, prophet of Jerusalem, historical icon, counselor of kings, still a household name over twenty centuries after he died, was first identified in Scripture simply as somebody's son, "the son of Amoz."

But who was Amoz? For that matter, what was Isaiah's mother's name? We don't know. Amazingly, we actually do know a bit about the woman to whom Isaiah himself was married. In Isaiah 8:3 she is referred to as a "prophetess," the mother of his children. Apparently she shared his religious vocation. In her own way, she, too, contributed to the spiritual leadership of God's people as a partner in delivering God's message to the people of Judah and Jerusalem.

Still, Isaiah's lineage remains obscure. Odds are, his family had clout. How else could Isaiah have had such access to address the royal court in the first place? How could he have become such an articulate critic of the social order of his day without a good education and the guided development of critical thinking skills? How could he have been protected from those in power who he admonished had he not had both social and religious standing and a significant support base in the local community? Even the prophetic language used by Isaiah—not unlike other prophets—was often the language a herald might use in making an announcement to a royal court in the ancient Near East. We can say with some certainty that Isaiah was a man of standing in his own day. He had identity and influence in his community, enhanced by longevity, prophesying during the reign of no less than four different kings! One could almost say that Isaiah was the Billy Graham of the eighth century BCE. As Billy Graham associated with every American president for more than half a century, so Isaiah did with the political leaders of his day, witnessing the rise and fall, triumphs and trials of the state.

Today Isaiah's identity is secure, no longer just as the son of Amoz. But being a son of Amoz was the start. His heritage established his place in the community, shaping much of his status, role, and future—as does our own personal heritage (though never entirely determinative). Of course, I and my fellow travelers did not end up in an isolated town in far-away Laos because of who are parents were. Or did we? Was it not their emotional and financial commitment to our education, not to mention their willingness to support a semester abroad in alien, war-torn South East Asia, that opened the doors for what followed (though they could hardly have imagined what we might actually get up to with such an opportunity!).

On that day in an old Asian capital, identity turned into opportunity. The man from Trent, delighted to discover a link to his own heritage in such a remote place, made us honored guests in his house, throwing a spontaneous feast to celebrate the occasion. Late that afternoon he even drove us to the small airport, got on a radio set in the small, metal-walled shack that served as a flight center, and called passing airplanes until he found the pilot of a small scout plane willing to fly us safely back to Vientiane, ultimately providing what became the most impressive memory of the trip. For, as the six-passenger Cessna lifted off the asphalt runway and looped upwards out of the valley, the setting sun lit the golden walls of the hilltop temple with a radiant glow and turned the Mekong river into a ribbon of gold shimmering below as twilight settled over the darkening, jungle-green mountains.

Identity matters. It establishes bonds and creates opportunities. As with Isaiah, so for us. Who we each are and what we will become for ourselves and to our community only unfolds over a lifetime. For us as for Isaiah, it starts with someone else—not only our parents, but all who went before us, the whole community that shapes us. It also includes a biblical prophet named Isaiah, son of Amoz.

For Discussion

1. Who have been the "identity-givers" in your life, the key people who have shaped who you are, from parents and siblings to teachers and strangers, and who have they helped you become?
2. How does your identity now impact the identity of others, for example, children, spouse, friends, co-workers, and others around you?

For Reflection

If you have a family tree, or just a picture of a parent, get it out and look it over. Think again about where you have come from—all the personalities and bloodlines and the swirling genetic pool that has manifested itself in the unique combination of atoms, DNA, and social molding that has made you, you. There is no one else quite the same. You can recall personal history, shaping moments, key influences, and what you might yet become. But do not forget to treasure what you already are and what your life already means to others, to God, and to yourself.

For Prayer

God who breathes us all into being, we marvel at the mystery of all the people and events that shape us. Teach us to treasure the gifts of identity and possibility that lie both within ourselves and in others. Amen.

4

Context

"In the days of Uzziah . . ."

ISAIAH 1:1C (RSV)

THERE IS A CATCHY 1970s song, written by Hoyt Axton and popularized by the band Three Dog Night, that begins, "Jeremiah was a bullfrog, was a good friend of mine . . ." (If you know this song, you can already hear it in your head.) Both rhythmically and conceptually, "Jeremiah was a Bullfrog" is considerably more engaging than "King Uzziah was a leper." Both Jeremiah and Uzziah are, of course, classic biblical names. The Old Testament Jeremiah was a prophet; Uzziah, a king of Judah.

Jeremiah, Uzziah, Judah, Jerusalem—biblical people, biblical places. Real people, real places. In other words, our friend Isaiah had a context:

> The vision of Isaiah, the son of Amoz,
> which he saw concerning Judah and
> Jerusalem in the days of Uzziah, Jotham,
> Ahaz, and Hezekiah, kings of Judah.
> Isaiah 1:1 (NRSV)

Context is everything. To fully appreciate the book of Isaiah, one would need to be well-versed in Near Eastern history and culture, biblical composition, the nature of prophetic writing, competing schools of theological thought in Israelite tradition, the historical progression of kings in Israel and Judah, etc. In other words, probably no one can *fully* appreciate Isaiah. But there are markers we all can use to help us appreciate the world in which Isaiah lived and to help us understand the impact of his life's work.

For one thing, Isaiah lived in tough times, much as we do. His was a world swirling with international intrigue, bloody conflicts, domestic rivalries, and deadly threats. In Isaiah's world fortunes often shifted with every new monarch. As in tales of medieval Europe, there were conspiracies and assassinations, pacts and betrayals. Walled cities and towered mini-kingdoms rose and fell by swinging sword and archer's arrow.

Superseding all the petty power struggles of the day was a far greater one: namely, the cosmic battle between faith and unbelief, in particular the struggle between faith in the God of Abraham and Sarah and belief in the myriad gods of the ancient Near East. To theologians such as Isaiah, the history of Israel and Judah was but a subplot in a far grander drama, the story of a God who not only authored human history but who got personally involved in its messy unfolding.

Uzziah, the first king under whom Isaiah served, succeeded in securing his kingdom in these turbulent times, at least for a while. His success contrasted starkly with Amazaiah, his father, and king before him, who got enmeshed in foolish personal rivalries, arrogantly dismissed his critics, abandoned the principles he was supposed to champion, and offended the very people he was supposed to serve to the point where they apparently hunted him down and crushed him with horses (2 Chronicles 25). Uzziah, on the other hand, became king at age sixteen with broad popular support, and, during his fifty-two year reign went on to consolidate and expand the kingdom of Judah into a position of considerable influence, prosperity, and renown throughout the region.

But what is especially intriguing about Uzziah are the unique details slipped into the biblical record of his reign. "He loved the soil," one text says (2 Chronicles 26:10). He "kept large herds," and supported a wine industry. With the help of smart managers, he was able to organize, fund, and equip a sizeable standing army for decades. Particularly intriguing is the unusual comment in Scripture that Uzziah "made engines, invented by skillful men" (2 Chronicles 26:15, RSV). Then, as today, military interests were often the driver for technological innovation. All these snippets paint a picture of a forward-thinking man of diverse interests, open to creative ideas.

Unfortunately, like so many such figures in literature and history, Uzziah's pride became his undoing. "But when he was strong, he grew proud, to his destruction. For he was false to the LORD his God . . ." (2 Chronicles 26:16, NRSV). Apparently, Uzziah assumed too much, trying to assert himself over the religious establishment of his day but discovering that the tides had turned. At the beginning of Uzziah's tale, "He did what was right in the eyes of the LORD . . . and as long as he sought the Lord, God made him prosper" (2 Chronicles 26:4a, 5b, RSV). But by the end of his life, he had strayed. His consequence was both visual and social. He became a marked man, a leper both medically and politically, removed from power, cut off from the society he had led to such achievement. This is the man whose ending signaled Isaiah's beginning, "In the year that King Uzziah died, I saw the LORD . . ." (Isaiah 6:1a, RSV).

Understanding begins with context.

For Discussion

1. What is your context? Who are the "kings" and nations that have shaped your life? Do you remember Martin Luther King's assassination? Who was the country's leader when you were born? What great issues and conflicts, what social upheavals and global events have you witnessed: 9/11? The Iraq War? The fall of the Berlin Wall? How did any or all of this affect you? In what ways have you been affected by such events that your children or those who come after you might never understand?
2. How do you think God has been speaking during these times? If you were called upon to identify God's presence in world events, what would you point to as an example? Or do you tend not to think in such terms?

For Reflection

Map the context of your life. Your map could take the shape of a timeline with key events or individuals. Perhaps you could draw a circle with yourself in the center, surrounded by people, places, and events. If you draw other circles next to yours for other people's contexts as well, you will soon have a massive inter-connected network of contexts, almost like cells in a living organism. In a culture committed to individuality, it can be thought-provoking to picture the contextual networks that surround us, each one an entity unto itself, yet intrinsically interdependent.

For Prayer

Lord of history, open our minds to perceive the deeper meanings of our times and the profound connections between our experiences and the ways you are present in them. Teach us to listen for your guiding word. Help us to make wiser choices in both our personal and our communal lives. Finally, give us the peaceful assurance that your history is destined for a graceful outcome. Amen.

5

The Heavens

"Hear, O heavens, and listen, O earth, for the Lord speaks."

ISAIAH 1:2A (NAB)

"*SHAMA SHAMAYIM*"—"HEAR, O HEAVENS." With these words Isaiah's prophecy begins. In some ways Isaiah's idea of the heavens was not so different from ours. For, together with earth, the visible heavens constituted the known universe for the early Hebrews. The Hubble telescope, string theory, and the many iterations of *Star Trek* and *Star Wars* all attest to the fascination we humans have with the cosmos in which we find ourselves. The biblical view, of course, is that behind the cosmic soup out of which earth and the heavens were drawn is a God who creates everything: "In the beginning God created the heavens and the earth" (Genesis 1:1). The very first words of the Bible present the Judaeo-Christian worldview.

There are alternative views. According to the Enuma Elish, an ancient Babylonian creation myth, a god named Marduk was the one who established the heavens and the earth. He did so by slitting open the belly of the malicious, bloated dragon Tiamat:

> "He split her up like a flat fish into two halves;
> one half of her he established as a covering for the heaven."
> Enuma Elish, tablet 4

The other half he laid out for the earth. Later, says the text, Marduk used his own blood to create human beings.

Nearly every culture in the world has some form of creation story, some way of explaining how the world came to be and how humans became part of it. From Amaterasu and the children of the sun in Japanese mythology to Ymir and Odin in Nordic culture, we humans have tried to explain our existence. It seems to be a unique aspect of being human that we pursue both origin and meaning. Something deep within us drives us to wonder where everything came from and why we are here. Fish do not think that way, as far as we know, or dogs or birds. So, why do we?

Yggdrasil: Tree of the Universe

There are some who would testify that such concerns obviously reflect an intelligent, spiritual foundation to life and the universe. Others would explain it as a sociological development, a survival mechanism, or an evolutionary brain function. To Isaiah, the explanation was simple, that is, God. For its time, the Hebrew idea of God was actually quite remarkable, specifically because of its simplicity: one God, a chosen people, and a historical struggle to cling to their God. Most other religions of the day had multiple gods, impersonal gods, a hierarchy of gods, and a host of ways and places to worship. Isaiah, together with other Hebrew prophets and teachers, was constantly wrestling with the forces pulling people away from the covenant God. Cultic and nationalistic gods have certainly always been common among human civilizations, but the Hebrew concept that the God who created the universe actually entered into human history and developed a permanent personal relationship with a particular group of people in a give-and-take relationship was part of what made the Hebrew faith so unique in the religious world of its day.

Isaiah's prophecy is based on that presumption. When Isaiah cries, "Hear O heavens, and listen O earth," he does so in the context of an assumed relationship. These words are just one excerpt from the "Great Conversation" that is continually going on between God and humanity in scripture. The first chapter of Isaiah presents that conversation in all the pain, frustration, and hope that characterize this particular moment in the history of God's relationship to humanity.

Interestingly enough, "Hear O heavens, and listen O earth" is also language reminiscent of a court scene. Like something out of prime-time television courtroom drama or perhaps an actual appeal to the Supreme Court, here is a formalized announcement of a legal case about to be argued. The Creator God is appealing to creation itself to witness to the charges about to be filed.

"Hear, O heavens and listen O earth" is the opening statement of a dialogue that is going to consume the entire ministry of Isaiah. It is a cosmic conversation that began long before he was born and which engages us yet today.

Ominous though that may sound, there is a saving grace in its very structure: "Hear O heavens, and listen O earth, *for the Lord speaks*" (italics added). The key lies in those last three words, "the Lord speaks." Isaiah's God was a speaking God, a God who communicates, a God who sends messengers and prophets, a God who keeps in touch. "Hear O heavens, and listen O earth" testifies to a cosmic drama that is unfolding as much in our day as it was in Isaiah's. For it is one thing to create a universe, another to stay involved in how it unfolds. But to go beyond that to the point of personally engaging in the lives and history of one struggling life form on a miniscule planet among a host of galaxies—that is another matter altogether. For us as for Isaiah, that is a matter worthy of our full attention.

For Discussion

1. Do gods create people, or do people create gods? Are you sometimes unsure? Why do you come down where you do?
2. Do you think of God as personal, as directly engaged in life's messy unfolding? Or are you more comfortable thinking of God in abstract terms, not unlike the deist founders of the United States, a god who put things in place and then lets us work out the daily details? Why do you lean towards one view or the other?

For Reflection

Go outside and look at the heavens, if you can, especially at night. You've marveled before at the expanse of the universe. Marvel again. Or go online to NASA's website or to a similar site with images of stars, planets, and spinning nebulae. Revel in the colors and grandeur. Then find a website or a book with a greatly magnified image of human tissue. Ponder the fact that the same kind of atomic particles which constitute the Milky Way and distant stars are found in your own body. We are all essentially stardust. What do you make of the utter integration of the cosmos?

For Prayer

God of all Galaxies, Star-Maker, draw us into your cosmic conversation. Attune our hearts to the rhythms of the universe so that we may hear your presence reverberating through energy and matter and hear your voice speaking through both prophet and neighbor. Transform our awe into action so that we may creatively contribute to the redemptive drama unfolding around us in the heavens and on earth. Amen.

6

The Speaking God

"For the LORD has spoken"

ISAIAH 1:2A (RSV)

DID YOU EVER WISH the person talking to you would just shut up? Maybe it's your kid in the back seat of the van recounting *ad nauseam* every minor detail about what each of their classmates said, ate, did, and threw during lunch time at school that day. Perhaps it's the gabby aunt who got a T-shirt for her birthday that said, "Help! I'm talking and I can't shut up!" and took it as a joke instead of the subtle message it was intended to be.

On the other hand, people usually wish that God would say more, not less. "Please, God, tell me what to do." "Explain how my sister's having terminal cancer is going to do her two young children any good."

It is natural to question God. Then again, is it? What gives us the impression that God is listening, that God cares, and that the God of the universe would bother with any individual human life anyway? Blame Isaiah, not to mention most of the rest of Scripture. For the God described by the Bible is, overall, a caring, communicative being. Perhaps we want God to say more precisely because we have grown accustomed to God's being so verbose. Or, we want God to say more because we have not actually been paying enough attention to what God has already said.

From the beginning of the Bible we are introduced to a speaking God. Ten times in just the first chapter of Genesis we read, "God said." Apparently, as soon as there is human consciousness, there is communication: "And God blessed them, and God said to them, 'Be fruitful . . .'" (Genesis 1:28a, RSV). After bringing order out of chaos, ordering light and darkness, and seeding an entire planet with biological life forms, God does not retreat into silence. Instead, the Creator starts a conversation with the ones created. Indeed, some of the most beautiful, provocative, promise-laden words in all of Scripture are spoken early in the Garden of Eden when God comes looking for Adam and Eve, calling out loud, "Where are you?" This image of a God who comes searching for us, speaking to us, inviting us into dialogue permeates the whole of Scripture, from Eden to Isaiah to Bethlehem. Isaiah assumed it. After all, the very premise of prophecy is that God communicates. The prophet is the messenger, the instrument through whom God's word resonates.

"Hear, O heavens and listen, O earth, for the LORD speaks" (Isaiah 1:2a, NAB). It is no accident that the first word of God's message via Isaiah is "hear," not "read." As biblical scholars would say, prophecy is by nature "oracular," an oral exchange between a source and a recipient in an interpersonal relationship. If God just wanted to hand out printed fliers or send mass emails or digital video to the people of earth, God could do that.

Of course, some would argue that God has done exactly that by providing the textual message called the Bible. But as Isaiah illustrates, that record itself is one of conversations, messages, and the insights that come from reflections on historical experiences of God's presence. Scripture is not meant to be a purely passive collection of essays to be objectively analyzed in the same way one would examine a scientific text book. Nor is Scripture meant to be read like a novel in a book club. The oracular intention of scripture is to engage us in a life-and-death conversation about what we believe and how we live.

The God conversation is not passive. When "the Lord speaks," whether through a dead prophet, a living person, or through the Holy Spirit, it is supposed to affect us. Most of all, God's speaking reveals God's character. For, the God who spoke through Isaiah is fundamentally a relational God. The kind of conversation we witness in Isaiah's prophecy is not just a "command and obey" communication system. It is a participatory exchange, where each party has a voice, where there is vulnerability on both sides.

What is extraordinary is that the God of all creation would choose to initiate such a conversational relationship in the first place. As witnessed by Isaiah's prophecy, the enduring image of the biblical God is one that transcends the punishments due a belligerent people. The God who warns of judgment is already a God in dialogue to deliver people from the disastrous outcomes of their decisions. In the end, it is the God who called creation good, the God who comes searching for us in the garden, the God who continually reaches out despite frustration and sometimes anger to love and bless us, the God who could not say more than what was expressed on a Roman cross. God has spoken. Isaiah calls us to listen.

For Discussion

1. How has God spoken to you? Via community? Conscience? The arts? If you never receive a direct, personal, indisputably divine-in-origin message, does it matter?
2. What would you most like to say to God right now?

For Reflection

Try silence. Set a time, find a place. Sit in a yogic meditation posture. Use breathing exercises if you know how. Or just sit in a chair and close your eyes. Identify what you hear, then focus on letting go of each sound, one at a time. Peel back the layers of distraction until you reach a calm, quiet core. Try to stay there as long as you can, even if for only a moment. Create room for a cosmic word to enter your being. Let God's Spirit speak. If words from Scripture help, let them flow and echo around your still space. Let yourself be drawn into God's life-giving conversation.

For Prayer

Speaking God, let your words flow into, through, and around us like a living stream, washing away the silt of self-centered being. Heighten our senses to pick up on the reverberations of your voice in scripture, in our relationships, and in the world around us. Deepen our listening so that we may more fully comprehend, appreciate and participate in this life-nourishing dialogue. Amen.

7

The Relational God

"I reared children and brought them up,
but they have rebelled against me."

ISAIAH 1:2B (NRSV)

His name hit the big city paper. The boy who once helped plant the neighborhood garden was going to jail. As an enthusiastic five-year-old, he had reveled in burying golden kernels of sweet corn seed in the rich, loamy soil. Squatting on his haunches with hands across his knees, he had stared expectantly at the quiet dirt, fascinated by the idea that a seed could just lie there in the dark until warmth and water caused it to explode into a new plant. Of course, he especially liked the part about how worms were down there tunneling through the soil, digesting leafy residue and pooping it out to make new dirt.

Now that boy for whom the world had held such wonder was headed for prison, far away from the therapeutic embrace of a summer garden. Mental demons had tormented his life as a young man, leading him to assault a police officer. Now he would be confined to a place of a different darkness, becoming a seed himself, buried in a steel and concrete womb, his loved ones hoping that warmth and light could penetrate his hardened shell to trigger new growth.

What does a parent do when a child "goes astray," when parental dreams are shattered, relationships ravaged, and when love isn't enough to protect the loved one or to prevent the march to self-destruction? There are days when you would lay down your life for the beloved if it would make a difference, alternating with days when you just want to throw up your hands in despair and walk away.

William Shakespeare's famous play *King Lear* tells the tale of two fathers undone by their own children. King Lear's two treacherous daughters sought not only to usurp his throne, but to kill each other, while his heroic, faithful, rejected daughter, Cordelia, met an untimely and cruel death after trying to rescue her father. The character called Gloucester, the King's loyal nobleman, was literally blinded by a heartless bastard son and left to die, saved only by his good son, whom he did not even recognize. In the play numerous tumultuous events unfold in the both literal and symbolic setting of a dark, dangerous forest and a wild English moor during a night of thunderstorms. By the end, both parents and several of the children are dead. King Lear has gone mad; the pain is unresolved; the future gloomy.

Shakespeare has nothing on Isaiah. Two thousand years before Shakespeare gave us King Lear, Isaiah recorded the agonizing words of another king: "I reared children and brought them up, but they have rebelled against me" (Isaiah 1:2b, NRSV). So broken is the relationship which Isaiah records that God's frustration expresses itself with an insult:

> The ox knows its owner, and the donkey its master's crib;
> but Israel does not know, my people do not understand.
> Isaiah 1:3 (NRSV)[

That's like saying, "My children are dumber than beasts; they can't even recognize their own master." God's frustration continues:

> Ah, sinful nation, people laden with iniquity,
> offspring who do evil, children who deal corruptly,
> who have forsaken the LORD,
> who have despised the Holy One of Israel,
> who are utterly estranged!
> Isaiah 1:4 (NRSV)

More than accusations, these words reveal deep parental grief.

To an Old Testament scholar these verses might be a poetic formula of echoing phrases, designed by an editor to reflect a ritualistic proclamation. But at a purely emotional level, these words reveal the heart of a wounded God, expressing the pain of rejection that can only come where an intimate relationship existed in the first place.

> Why do you seek further beatings?
> Why do you continue to rebel?
> The whole head is sick, and the whole heart faint.

> From the sole of the foot even to the head,
> there is no soundness in it,
> but bruises and sores and bleeding wounds;
> they have not been drained, or bound up, or softened with oil.
> Isaiah 1:5–6 (NRSV)

How bad do things have to get, the parent laments, before you come to your senses? Your life is a wreck. You hurt inside and out. Your future is forfeit; your enemies have triumphed. Put in modern terms, the banks and courts, the psychiatrists and attorneys, the police and the media—these are the ones who will call the shots for your life now. What is it going to take to get through to you?

From this point on in the book of Isaiah, we know what it is going to be about. Ultimately, it is a love story, a dramatic, vivid family saga about estrangement and betrayal, the offspring's misdirected, doomed struggles for independence, contrasted with God's intense desire for reconciliation and new beginnings. All the usual dramatic ingredients are present: anger, threats, promises, pleas, rebellion and redemption. The first chapter of Isaiah becomes the canvas upon which is painted the backdrop for the complex drama to follow. As the scenes unfold and players enter and exit the stage, will the saga descend into the discordant darkness of Shakespeare's *King Lear*? Or, will it wind towards an uplifting resolution? Or both?

For Discussion

1. From whom have you been estranged in your life, especially in your own family? Recall a phase in your life that was overly "self-absorbed," focused on shaping your own preferred direction in life, distanced from the context in which you were raised. What was lost? What was gained? Did your experience or understanding of God change?
2. How does pain affect faith? How does faith affect pain?

For Reflection

Imagine darkness: Lear wandering the stormy moor, blind Gloucester stumbling through the forest, being in the woods by yourself at night when your flashlight dies, or just trying to find your way around a darkened house when the electricity has gone off. Now picture a flicker of light in the distance. Feel the relief, the reassurance that you will regain direction—even control—that you will return to safety, normality, redemption. It takes so little light to counter the ever-threatening darkness.

For Prayer

Source of all Light, be our beacon when we get lost in the forests of failure, flawed choices, damaged relationships, and self-serving behaviors. Reconnect us with those we need to love and those who already love us. Penetrate the soil of our dormant spirits with your warmth, light, and life-giving water, so that we may become seeds of possibility. This we pray. Amen.

8

The Nepalese Goat

"What to me is the multitude of your sacrifices? says the Lord;
I have had enough of burnt offerings of rams and the fat of fed beasts;
I do not delight in the blood of bulls, or of lambs, or of he-goats.
When you come to appear before me,
who requires of you this trampling of my courts?
Bring me no more vain offerings: incense is an abomination to me.
New moons and Sabbath and the calling of assemblies—
I cannot endure iniquity and solemn assembly.
Your new moons and your appointed feasts my soul hates;
they have become a burden to me, I am weary of bearing them.
When you spread forth your hands, I will hide my eyes from you;
even though you make many prayers, I will not listen;
Your hands are full of blood.
Wash yourselves; make yourselves clean;
remove the evil of your doings from before my eyes;
cease to do evil, learn to do good;
seek justice, correct oppression; defend the fatherless;
plead for the widow . . ."
Isaiah 1:11–17 (RSV)

We stood transfixed, peering over the low stucco wall at the impending slaughter. The Nepalese holidays were in full swing, which explained all the chickens and goats we had seen being herded down streets into the city. Jean Claude, my French traveling companion, and I had been wandering the back streets of Kathmandu as religious voyeurs, witnessing the ancient ritual of animal sacrifice. In one street we had watched as a goat was offered up, its blood sprinkled with prayers over the engine of a new Toyota pickup truck, its severed head ensconced on the vehicle's bumper and ringed with garlands of flowers.

By the time we passed the small courtyard of a family home where a priest was sprinkling a goat—flagon of water in one hand, blade in the other—we had figured out that the goat must shake three times, once after each anointing, in order for the sacrifice to proceed. The reluctant goat in the courtyard reacted very slowly to the second sprinkling; the family and priest seemed at first impatient, then worried, then reassured as the goat finally shivered. When the third sprinkling was met with indifference, and the family glanced our way, we realized that our presence as outsiders might be seen as interfering with the sacred flow of the ancient ritual for the blessing of this household. Immediately we turned away and moved on, but glanced back briefly, relieved—for the family, not for the goat—to see the goat shiver a third time.

The Old Testament is virtually awash with the blood of animal sacrifice. God used it to seal the covenant with Abraham (Genesis 15:7–11, 17–21). In Egypt sacrificial blood on the doorposts saved the Israelites from the Angel of Death. For centuries the temple sacrifices in Jerusalem were a central element of worship for God's chosen people. Even Jesus took part, both as a child and as an adult. Only with the Roman destruction of the second temple in 70 CE did the practice finally diminish. For Christians it is no coincidence that at that same point in human history another sacrifice took place which rendered all others both insufficient and fulfilled. But Christians, as well as Jews, then had to reconceive the nature and basis of worship, a process which remains in flux to this day. For Isaiah, obviously, worship was a serious matter:

> Hear the word of the Lord, you rulers of Sodom;
> listen to the law of our God, you people of Gomorrah!
> "The multitude of your sacrifices—what are they to me?"
> says the Lord;
> "I have more than enough of burnt offerings, of rams and the fat
> of fattened animals; I have no pleasure in the blood of bulls
> and lambs and goats."
> Isaiah 1:10–11 (NIV)

The gravity of these words reflects the degree of estrangement between God and God's people. In Isaiah's day after all, how scary would it have been to hear that the supreme object of your devotion, the One who you are trying to please, completely rejects your religious efforts?! On top of that, to be called "people of Gomorrah," was to be ranked with the most despicable class of "rejects" imaginable, people considered to be so far from God that they had to be obliterated. Up to this point, no matter how bad things had got for the people of Israel, no matter how much God's people had messed up, there was always the one symbolic group to whom they could compare themselves and over against whom they could feel self-righteous. No more. Not even their elaborate public piety could cover up the problem.

> When you come to appear before me,
> who has asked this of you, this trampling of my courts?
> Stop bringing meaningless offerings!
> Your incense is detestable to me.
> Isaiah 1:12–13a (NIV)

A few chapters later in Isaiah incense is a symbol of mystery, an expression of the ineffable presence of God, a representation of fragrant offerings and prayers. But at this point it is just a smoke screen for hypocritical behavior.

> New Moons, Sabbaths and convocations—
> I cannot bear your evil assemblies.
> Your New Moon festivals and your appointed feasts my soul hates.
> They have become a burden to me; I am weary of bearing them.
> Isaiah 1:13b–14 (NIV)

Apparently, even God knows what it is like to have to attend yet one more over-hyped, over-done religious event.

The real issue, of course, is the disconnect between the form of religion and its content, between empty words and transforming deeds. ("So faith by itself, if it has no works, is dead," James 2:17, RSV.) When worship becomes mere public display or self-righteous posturing, when it exists for its own sake or primarily for the gratification of the worshipers and/or worship leaders, it loses its soul. When worship devolves into ritualistic appeasement, it is clear that the relationship that gave rise to it in the first place is in jeopardy.

Understandably, all of this can be discouraging to worship specialists, the professional class of modern-day priests and scholars, musicians, and officiants in congregations today. For too many of them—as well as for many worshipers—the form of worship is itself the content. There is a sense that if worship is done "right" according to traditions, or, on the other hand, that if worship is done with sufficient emotive expression, then one's religious work is done and God is duly gratified.

No wonder Isaiah's words are disturbing. They hit where it hurts. Moreover, the discomfort is intensified by the dramatically "anthropomorphic" or personalized way in which God's reaction is presented:

> "*I* have had enough . . .When you come to appear before *me*,
> who requires of you this trampling of *my* courts? . . .
> *I* cannot endure iniquity and solemn assembly.
> Your new moons and your appointed feasts *my* soul hates;
> they have become a burden to *me*, *I* am weary of bearing them.
> When you spread forth your hands, *I* will hide *my* eyes from you;
> even though you make many prayers, *I* will not listen."
> Isaiah 1:11–15b (RSV, italics added)

This very personal, emotional language is actually a mirror image of the emotional, personal experience that so many of us desire to have in worship. Ironically, it is the lack of genuine personal investment that is portrayed here by highlighting the emptiness of purely ritualistic worship.

Remarkably, for nearly two thousand years most Christians have followed the so-called Latin or Western Rite, that rich tradition by which worship is organized into component parts ranging from the Salutation ("The Lord be with you . . .") to the eucharistic Sanctus ("Holy, holy, holy") to the dismissal (*Missa ite est* . . . from which the English reference to the "Mass" derives).

In its various forms and multiple musical expressions this tradition has served to unify Christians around the world and across the centuries in a common worship experience and even with a common religious language (literally so with the Latin Mass). It has in large measure contributed to an orthodoxy of Christian belief, focusing the worshiping community on the central tenets of Christian faith. Along the way, the Western rite has given rise to some of the most lavish and beautiful art and music in human history.

How intriguing then, that in the current historical era, Christians are abandoning this tradition by the millions. Arguably, the majority of practicing Christians in the world today—as apparent among Christians in Africa, China, and among Evangelicals in North and South America as well as in Europe—already are or soon will be worshiping in alternative liturgical styles.

What are we to make of that phenomenon in terms of Isaiah's message? Does it reflect what Isaiah addresses—a change in focus from ritualistic to personal engagement? Or is it a reflection of modern, individualistic culture, at least in the West, where organizational loyalties have declined, where community-based identities are undermined, where people are searching for personal meaning through a more direct connection with the divine? Or will the opposite prove true, namely that this trend will reverse itself, and that traditional forms will again become more important for social cohesion, community building, and for cultivating common ground?

Either way, worship will almost surely remain the visible means by which communities of believers organize and express their relationship to ultimate reality. That response may be fear-based, obedience-orientated, love-rooted, or whatever, but will inevitably include ritual. The question is: will it become the kind of worship described by Isaiah? Isaiah's words, after all, call us back to the source, to the foundation and the reason for doing worship in the first place—namely, as an act of relationship. At its best, worship is a language the heart speaks. Ritual, symbol, music, and sensation carry us beyond what our words can express. The question is: to what are we transported? God's anthropomorphic language is an invitation back to intimacy, to the loving embrace of a meaningful, fulfilling, respectful relationship with the original author of all our worship.

For Discussion

1. What does worship do for you? What styles of worship most inspire, feed you, or best enable you to honor God? What rituals are especially meaningful to you? When you recall worship experiences from your childhood, what key features and memories emerge? What feelings accompany those memories?
2. To what extent is it important to participate in worship for the sake of the community, preserving tradition and adjusting to what "works" for others even if it does not work for you?

For Reflection

Go to worship. Simply close your eyes and imagine yourself sitting in the space where you usually worship. Focus on the sights, smells, sounds, colors and sensations. Here is where you gather with others to invest a piece of your life in worship. Why do you do that? Is it just habit? Are you seeking inspiration? Consolation? Companionship in your faith journey? Peace? All of that and more?

Now consider God's point of view (as much as a human can). What does God want out of your worship? What do you do just to honor the relationship, to show praise, awe, thanksgiving? How often is your offering from your heart? How often do you leave worship feeling cleansed, renewed, recharged, and inspired for pursuing the life you have been given?

Find a small object—a cross, a Bible, a smooth stone, a picture, beads, or whatever. Hold it in your hand and physically lift it as an offering before God, as a point of connection from your heart. Imagine that God receives it and says, "Yes."

For Prayer

Loving God, origin of our heart's longing for communion with you, saturate us with your presence. Direct our worship towards both substance and service, free from self-serving distractions. Teach us both to treasure and to employ the rich resources of worship traditions sanctified by centuries of faithful practice.

Enlighten us that we may understand worship as more than a merely personal act, but one which draws us more deeply into you through our life in unity with others. May worship sustain and support us in witness to your presence in the wider world and in service to those with whom we share it.

Let your Spirit steer us towards that day when history's unfolding will be complete and the universe will explode into praise, when together with neighbors, angels and stars we will participate in the fulfillment of eternity's perfect worship. Amen.

9

Molech

"Your hands are full of blood; wash and make yourselves clean."

ISAIAH 1:15C, 16A (NIV)

"OUT, DAMNED SPOT! OUT, I say!" These words, from William Shakespeare's play *Macbeth* (act 5, scene 1) have been an idiom in the English language for nearly 400 years. In the play, the duplicitous Lady Macbeth, after helping to assassinate the rightful king, imagines that her hands are still stained with his blood. Driven by encroaching madness, she is observed sleepwalking through the castle, trying to rub the bloody spot from her hands.

A more modern take on this famous theme appears in the 2006 James Bond movie, *Casino Royale* (Sony Pictures). There, the leading lady slumps fully clothed under a cold running shower, staring at her hand, distraught by the imaginary blood spilled on it in a fatal encounter with yet another detestable villain recently dispatched by her heroic defender, the famous British spy. Isaiah should get at least a footnote reference from both Bond and the Bard. For, Isaiah said it first, "Your hands are full of blood" (Isa. 1:15b). What did he mean?

In the clan conflicts, ethnic cleansings, and regional battles of Isaiah's world, slaughter was pervasive. Ascension to political office was as commonly achieved by assassination as by divine appointment. But perhaps the most heinous expression of these bloody times was the gruesome ritual of child sacrifice. Throughout the Middle East from at least the time of Abraham (and perhaps reflected in the story of Abraham's near sacrifice of Isaac) right down to the time of Jesus, 2000 years later, this abominable religious ritual persisted. Ahaz, king of Israel in Isaiah's day, apparently burned his own sons to death in the fires of Molech, as did Manasseh, another Israelite king (2 Chronicles 28:3 and 2 Kings 21:6).

Molech, the god for whom these children were slaughtered, remains a mysterious figure in biblical history, known by different names in different cultures. But, emerging from this repulsive mystery of the past comes a question to haunt modern believers. Namely, is Molech still with us?

Martin Luther defined a god as that which we value above all else, particularly as demonstrated by our actions. In that sense we may ask, do human deeds today describe a living Molech, a driving force in our world that commands our allegiance to the point of offering up our own children in sacrifice to it? When parents in the Middle East dress up their toddlers in military camouflage, put toy guns in their hands and strap fake suicide belts to their waist before snapping pictures of them for others to see, does this reflect a Molech mentality? When children in developing countries are sold into indentured servitude to spend ten hours a day weaving rugs or making trinkets for sale by international corporations to first world consumers, is not the spirit of Molech present? Terrorist attacks that blow apart children and adults indiscriminately are almost by definition a manifestation of the Molech syndrome. Even laser-guided bombs that unintentionally kill children carry the stain of Molech. When tens of thousands of children a year are forced to become child soldiers in guerrilla or ethnic wars, is not Molech being served? In such a context God's call through Isaiah's words becomes even more poignant.

> "Wash and make yourselves clean.
> Take your evil deeds out of my sight!
> Stop doing wrong,
> Learn to do right."
> Isaiah 1:16–17a (NIV)

God provides another option, so that Molech will not prevail,

> "Seek justice, encourage the oppressed.
> Defend the cause of the fatherless
> Plead the case of the widow."
> Isaiah 1:17 (NIV)

Throughout Scripture and especially with the prophets we see what God has in mind for how human beings are supposed to treat each other. As we discover repeatedly in Isaiah's legacy, the biblical record describes a God with a heart for justice, not blood. In complete contrast to the mind of Molech which continues to wreak havoc in the human community, the mind of Isaiah's God is directed towards compassion, justice, redemption, and restoration.

In one of the most extraordinary and encouraging phrases in all of Scripture God says "Come now, let us reason together" (Isaiah 1:18, NIV). What kind of God invites mortals into a two-way dialogue, offering mutual respect and a willingness to listen to the opinions of partners who have so vividly demonstrated a complete disregard for reasonable behavior and justice? What does it say about us that God's words assume we have a functioning sense of reason to which to appeal? That reason exists, that justice and compassion are even human options—woven into the very fabric of what it means to be human—is a remarkable revelation about God. The God who becomes so upset with our actions—as illustrated by the account in the remainder of this chapter about how God's people have corrupted their government and ignored the needy in their community—is a God who intends something far better for humanity.

> "I will thoroughly purge away your dross
> and remove all your impurities.
> I will restore your judges as in days of old, your counselors as at the beginning . . .
> Zion will be redeemed with justice . . ."
> Isaiah 1:25b, 26a, 27a (NIV)

God's passion is for the redemption and up-building of the human community, not its destruction. That is the whole point of prophets and Scripture. However, as the prophets consistently make clear, when humanity chooses a contrary path, the consequences are severe. God will do whatever is necessary to turn things around.

> Rebels and sinners will both be broken,
> and those who forsake the Lord will perish . . .
> "You will be ashamed . . .
> You will be disgraced . . ."
> Isaiah 1:28, 29 (NIV)

Human self-reliance is a futile enterprise. It leads to dry, unrelieved emptiness. In the end we are given a choice. We can wander the way of Molech, either by ignorance or intent. Or we can pursue the path of the prophets.

For Discussion

1. Why does Molech have such power and appeal? Where have you witnessed the effect of Molech in your own life?
2. What can you do today—even a simple, specific act—to oppose the impact of "Molech-ular" influence in the world and to help restore someone or something?

For Reflection

Troubling though it may be, let some of the awful images you have seen on TV surface in your mind: burned out villages in Darfur, the carnage of Iraqi car bombs, the piles of skulls in Rwanda or Cambodia, the roiling clouds of death-laden smoke and dust from the Twin Towers on 9/11. Let down the protective barriers; release the senses numbed by too many horrific images. What emerges within you? Tears? Anger? Fear? Be reassured for having them. They are a healthy sign of something within you that still recognizes evil, injustice, and the world of Molech. Pray for those who are so callous that they feel nothing.

Now picture the world as you would like it to be: safe, no one left out or put down or exploited, a world where no children are sacrificed to destructive agendas. But consider the possibility that what you picture may be limited by your own culturally defined perspective. Try to imagine what God's greater vision might be. Remember Eden? The wolf and the lamb? A new heaven and earth where no tears are shed? Imagine what that might look like in the world today.

For Prayer

Restoring God, deliver us from Molech, not only Molech in the world around us but also the nascent Molech tendencies within each one of us. Strengthen the capacity for reason and compassion which you have implanted in humankind, so that we may discern and resist destructive religious, political, and economic ideologies. Deliver us from blind trust in human institutions, even religious ones, which can also manifest the insidious influence of Molech. Help us to understand and accept chastening as a step toward our healing and restoration. Finally, move our hearts to a deep, biblical mindfulness of those among us who are in need of protection, assistance, and justice. Enable us to be advocates for and partners in your redemptive, restorative work. Amen.

10

The Torah from Al Aqsa

"This is what Isaiah son of Amoz saw concerning Judah and Jerusalem:
In the last days the mountain of the LORD's temple
will be established as chief among the mountains;
it will be raised above the hills, and all nations will stream to it."

ISAIAH 2:1–2 (NIV)

AL AQSA IS THE name of the great Muslim mosque compound that sits atop Mt. Moriah in Jerusalem. This is probably not what Isaiah pictured in his prophecy. Then again, prophecy does not always play out as expected. In some ways, however, Isaiah's vision has been fulfilled far beyond anything he could have imagined. According to Israel's Ministry of Foreign Affairs, more than a million people a year now "stream to" Jerusalem. Most of them visit the temple mount, historic site of "the Lord's temple," which in Isaiah's day was the temple built by King Solomon. Utterly destroyed by the Romans in 70 CE, the temple grounds later became the fabled site of Mohammed's night journey into heaven from atop the giant rock upon which Abraham had almost sacrificed Ishmael (according to Muslim teaching). By the sixth century of the Christian Era, the exquisite Dome of the Rock had been erected, and Al Aqsa had become the second oldest and third most holy site in Islam. Countless postcards, panoramic photographs and aerial videos have since carried the image of the beautiful gold-domed, blue mosaic shrine around the world, making it as iconic a symbol of Jerusalem as the Eiffel Tower is to Paris or the Statue of Liberty is to New York.

Almost as widely photographed and disseminated are images of the Western Wall, the massive retaining wall supporting the grounds of Al Aqsa. Built by King Herod not long before Jesus was born, the wall is made of expertly chiseled limestone blocks, some of which are even larger than those used in the Pyramids of Egypt.

In 1967, during the Six Day War, when Israeli paratroopers fought their way street-by-street through the Old City of Jerusalem (under orders to avoid damage to ancient structures) the Western Wall was one of their primary objectives. Guns in hand, bloodied, and still exposed to hostile fire, the soldiers pushed to the Wall, celebrating, weeping, and praying at the holiest site in Judaism.

In the Fall of 2000 on the grounds of Al Aqsa just above the Wall, the second Palestinian Intifada began, young Muslims taking to the streets with stones and guns, outraged over what they saw as a provocative intrusion by an Israeli politician into the sacred space of Al Aqsa.

Was this what Isaiah had in mind? That the nations of the world would "stream to the mountain of the Lord," guns blazing, cameras rolling, the world watching on TV, the United Nations and world governments sending plane load after plane load of diplomats, presidents, and politicians to address the perpetually vexing problem of to whom the mountain of the Lord really belonged? (Isaiah knew.) Did Isaiah envision the busloads of Japanese, American, and European tourists streaming into Jerusalem, along with countless scholars, pilgrims, and photojournalists? Surely not! What Isaiah envisioned was far more spectacular:

> Many peoples will come and say,
> "Come, let us go up to the mountain of the
> LORD, to the house of the God of Jacob. He will teach us his ways,
> so that we may walk in his paths." The law will go out from Zion,
> the word of the LORD from Jerusalem.
> He will judge between the nations and will settle disputes
> for many peoples.
> Isaiah 2:3–4a (NIV)

Isaiah prophesied two great futures for humanity stemming from this central spiritual place: understanding and peace. The Torah, the law, the teaching of God would emanate from "the mountain of the Lord," enabling humanity to find a way forward on its perilous journey, a way that would include all people. Often in Old Testament literature and culture the phrase "the nations" (*ha-goyim* in Hebrew) was a term of discrimination, exclusive, even contemptuous. But here the idea is just the opposite: harmony, connection, and the resolution of differences between peoples.

For some, this implies all peoples being converted to a common faith or identical point of view, and implicitly, it at least suggests finding common ground. But could the holiness of the mountain of the Lord to Muslim, Jew, and Christian alike be itself a metaphor for the realization of Isaiah's message? Can the Torah, the instruction of God, be more comprehensive than yet understood? Here we are, Christians, Muslims and Jews, two thousand seven hundred years after Isaiah prophesied, learning from each other as never before, engaged in a conversation—sometimes volatile and even dangerous—that affects every person on the planet. Stress and fear tend to intensify this conversation. But what if we take courage from Isaiah's words:

> "He shall judge between the nations
> and shall arbitrate for many peoples;
> they shall beat their swords into plowshares, and their spears into pruning hooks;
> nation shall not lift up sword against nation;
> neither shall they learn war anymore."
> Isaiah 2:4 (NRSV)

Was Isaiah just a foolish dreamer? Or can we find hope for our times in the images he offers? The opening words of Isaiah's prophecy refer to "the last days," a time when history's purpose will be realized, a future already being born, often via pain. But the overwhelming good news of Isaiah is that God's intended future is extraordinarily positive. With humanity's heart-rending record of conflict and injustice it is hard to imagine a world where nations disarm and weapons are transformed into instruments for cultivating order and prosperity. Yet here stands Isaiah's breathtaking vision, offering phenomenal hope to a divided world. Whether Muslim, Buddhist, Christian, Hindu, or Jew, who cannot be captured by such a dream? Even those who claim no faith can respond positively to the vision that "neither shall they learn war anymore." (Isaiah 2:4b, RSV)

For Discussion

1. Is Al Aqsa the Lord's temple?
2. Do you subscribe to the view that in the end one religion will reign supreme over all others as the "right" representation of God's Word? Why? Or why not?

For Reflection

Ponder holiness. What physical places in your life are infused with a sense of the holy, whatever you perceive that to be? Which of those places do you share with others?

Ask yourself: where do you find Torah, instruction so that you can walk in the ways of the Lord? Where else could you look?

Reflect on your key relationships: are you carrying any swords that would better be molded into plowshares, attitudes, resentments, or anger that could be redirected towards reconciliation and peace?

For Prayer

God of all nations, lead us to your temple. Instruct us in the ways we should go. Fill us with the vision of a world at peace. Open our hearts and minds to all the peoples and nations with whom we share this journey, and teach us all how to transform the tools of conflict into instruments of healing. Amen.

11

Enron and the Floozies of Jerusalem

"The LORD has taken his place to contend, he stands to judge his people."

ISAIAH 3:13 (RSV)

"ENRON" HAS BECOME PART of America's vocabulary. The rise and fall of this Texas energy conglomerate has become an iconic tale of greed, deception, and collapse. Hundreds of hard-working people were damaged by the manipulation of public assets for private gain; many lost their life's savings. More recently, the 2008 credit collapse in world markets, from overextended mortgage firms to overleveraged investment banks, damaged countless homeowners and investors, threatening at least a partial collapse of the entire global economy.

In Isaiah's time there were comparable cases of financiers who prospered at the expense of others. In fact, Isaiah's accounts describe a class of people who led lives not unlike the elite of Enron and Wall Street: "Their land is full of silver and gold; there is no end to their treasures" (Isaiah 2:7a, NIV).

In modern times the wealthy class has exploded, not only in the United States but around the world. Recently-communist China now boasts over a million millionaires, with new ones being added daily. Over 8 percent of American households hold assets of a million dollars or more, even while the income of the average American family has declined annually for nearly a decade in terms of actual purchasing power. Among the upper class of various Gulf States, wealth is measured in "deca-millions" rather than in single millions. The mega-wealthy of Europe spent millions of dollars just for luxury yacht berths in Valencia, Spain in 2007 in order to watch a week-long America's Cup race. Orders for yachts valued at ten million dollars or more were up 18 percent in 2008 and spiked again in 2010. In Africa a recent offer of a five million dollar prize each year to outstanding government leaders was met with skepticism because so many leaders there can skim significantly more out of government coffers for personal use.

No wonder the general public relishes "perp walks," the televised spectacle of rich corporate or political titans being escorted in handcuffs to jail. Whether born of a sense of injustice or rooted in jaded jealousy, the average person tends to take a certain pleasure at seeing the wealthy classes brought down a peg or two. Isaiah knew how to play this penchant of ours exceptionally well.

> The Lord Almighty has a day in store for all the proud and lofty . . .
> The arrogance of man will be brought low and the pride of men humbled;
> the LORD alone will be exalted in that day,
> and the idols will totally disappear.
> Isaiah 2:12a, 17, 18 (NIV)

So offended was God, according to Isaiah, that Isaiah said to God, "You have abandoned your people" (Isaiah 2:6a). Excess, idolatry, arrogance, and the pursuit of military might (horses and chariots: Isaiah 2:7b) are named as the reason. But which came first? Were the choices and values of this society a cause of their abandonment by God, or were they a consequence, simply a sign of what happens when a society starts believing that its destiny is purely in its own hands? How does a society know when it has crossed the line, when its moral, economic, and political character auger its doom? Ask the survivors of Stalinist Russia, Hitler's Germany, or Hirohito's Japan. Even they might not have an answer. What is unmistakably clear, however, are the devastating consequences of destructive human ideologies.

In Kampuchea (Cambodia) between 1975 and 1979 as many as two million people—one-fourth of the population—were slaughtered. In a society gone mad, chaos reigned, cities were emptied, people could be killed for wearing eye glasses or showing emotion as a family member was put to death in front of them. Although the context and cause was far different in Jerusalem in the eighth century BCE, Isaiah's description of life there during the decline of the Kingdom of Judah has elements in common with what happened under the Khmer Rouge.

> And the people shall oppress one another,
> yes, every man his neighbor.
> The child shall be bold toward the elder,
> and the base toward the honorable . . .
> O my people, your leaders mislead,
> they destroy the paths you should follow.
> Isaiah 3:5, 12b (NAB)

What happened in Cambodia echoed the Cultural Revolution in China during the 1960s, when young Maoists led their elders through the streets in dunce caps, when the government closed universities, tore families apart, and shipped off to labor camps (or worse) anyone whose education and skilled leadership represented a threat to the state ideology.

In Isaiah's world the Assyrians and later the Babylonians perpetrated such policies on a grand scale. After depriving conquered people of all but the basics for survival, they stripped off the leadership layers of both Israel's and Judah's societies and either killed or exiled anyone with the skills or will to resist.

> The Lord, the Lord of hosts,
> shall take away from Jerusalem and from Judah
> support and prop [all supplies of bread and water]:
> Hero and warrior,
> judge and prophet, fortuneteller and elder,
> The captain of fifty and the nobleman,
> counselor, skilled magician, and expert charmer.
> I will make striplings their princes;
> the fickle shall govern them . . .
> Isaiah 3:1–5 (NAB)

Though the Assyrians and Babylonians were the instruments of this gruesome gleaning, Isaiah and other prophets understood God to be the actual author of such historical events, designed, as they were, to punish God's people for their errant ways and to cleanse them for a new beginning.

> The Lord rises to accuse,
> standing to try his people.
> The LORD enters into judgment with his people's elders and princes:
> It is you who have devoured the vineyard;

> the loot wrested from the poor is in your houses.
> What do you mean by crushing my people,
> and grinding down the poor when they look to you?
> Isaiah 3:13–15 (NAB)

Excess and exploitation are met with judgment. The Isaiah paradigm precedes the Enron paradigm by more than 2500 years. The prophets' message (not only Isaiah, but also Amos, Micah, Habakkuk and others) was that the God who expects justice will not in the end tolerate a society without it.

Perhaps it is more than greed that fuels our suspicion of excessive wealth. Could it be that embedded deep in the human psyche, as the prophetic writings portray, there is a fundamental instinct for economic balance and fairness? For the believer, the injustice archetype decreed by the God of Scripture is as applicable in modern times as it was in Isaiah's day. To drive home his point, Isaiah targeted an unusual constituency:

> The Lord said:
> Because the daughters of Zion are haughty,
> and walk with necks outstretched
> Ogling and mincing as they go,
> their ankles tinkling with every step,
> The Lord shall cover the scalps of Zion's daughters with scabs,
> and the Lord shall bare their heads.
> On that day the Lord will do away with the finery of the anklets,
> sunbursts, and crescents, the pendants, bracelets, and veils;
> the headdresses, bangles, cinctures, perfume boxes,
> and amulets; the signet rings, and the nose rings;
> the court dresses, wraps, cloaks, and purses;
> the mirrors, linen tunics, turbans, and shawls.
> Isaiah 3:16–24 (NAB)

Why did Isaiah pick on the women of Jerusalem in an almost Taliban-like manner? What does it suggest about Isaiah that he paid so much attention to the fashions, make-up, and hair styles of his day that he could provide us with such a detailed description? Clearly, the fashion industry was alive and well three millennia before Calvin Klein, Yves St. Laurent, and Victoria's Secret! But this passage is about more than Isaiah's skills as a social commentator. Nor does it likely stem simply from a prejudice against women or from an unhappy love life. Rather, Isaiah's focus on the upper class women of Jerusalem, "ogling and mincing as they go" amplifies the "shock value" of his whole message. As wealth rises to the top in exploitative society, fashion and material displays are obvious expressions of that and offer a useful tool for conveying the impending collapse of an illusion: "Instead of perfume there will be stench, instead of the girdle, a rope, and for the coiffure, baldness; for the rich gown, a sackcloth skirt" (Isaiah 3:24, NAB). As the Revised Standard Version translates it, "the Lord will lay bare their secret parts" (Isaiah 3:17b) when the downfall of their society arrives. No one can accuse Isaiah of lacking a flair for the dramatic. His images give prophetic imagination a whole new meaning.

In the end, Isaiah is simply setting up his audience with the tried and true technique of a "carrot and stick" approach. The stick of destruction is real; it is coming and it is going to hurt—a lot. But then will come the carrot. Devastation is not the end. The end, as Isaiah proclaims, is deliverance.

> On that day, the branch of the Lord shall be beautiful and glorious,
> and the fruit of the land shall be the pride and glory
> of the survivors of Israel.
> Whoever is left in Zion and remains in Jerusalem will be called holy,
> everyone who has been recorded for life in Jerusalem,
> once the LORD has washed away the filth of the daughters of Zion
> and cleansed the bloodstains of Jerusalem from its midst
> by a spirit of judgment and by a spirit of burning.
> Then the LORD will create over the whole site of Mount Zion
> and over its places of assembly a cloud by day,
> and smoke and the shining of a flaming fire by night.
> Indeed over all the glory there will be a canopy.
> It will serve as a pavilion,
> a shade by day from the heat,
> and a refuge and a shelter from the storm and rain.
> Isaiah 4:2–6 (NRSV)

Anyone familiar with the story of the Exodus—even if only from the Cecil B. DeMille movie *The Ten Commandments*—will recognize Isaiah's smoking cloud and flaming fire by its reference. The cloud by day and fire by night were the symbols of God's deliverance and protective presence as the Israelites fled Egypt on their way to the Promised Land. Isaiah's encouragement is that when the chastening is done, the consequences played out, God stands ready to start anew with those who will listen. In the end, the people are not abandoned, but redeemed.

For Discussion

1. Would you agree that there is a fundamental sense of justice embedded in human consciousness? If so, does it come from God, or is it simply an evolutionary survival mechanism?
2. Is the "Day of the Lord" with its judgment for both injustice and faithfulness a comforting image or a disturbing one? How so?

For Reflection

What appears in your mind when you picture excess—grand mansions, luxury cars, yachts . . . ? Which feeling is strongest in you: disdain, indifference, envy? What appears in your mind when you picture poverty—the distended bellies of starving children, people picking through garbage dumps for food, families crowded into tents or dilapidated apartments? Which feeling is strongest in you: numbness, despair, outrage? Now marvel at and celebrate the billions of dollars and endless hours that ordinary individuals are constantly donating to relieve the suffering of their fellow human beings, especially in times of natural disasters. Celebrate the human capacity for doing good, from individual acts of selfless kindness to the innumerable organizations created for helping both people and the planet. Ponder the interplay between exploitation and compassion.

For Prayer

Justice-seeking God, deliver us from idols and ideologies that lead to destruction. In societies where chaos reigns may deliverance come. Where exploitation and excess corrupt human community may there be recompense and reform. Teach us to balance our lives and our societies with justice and a recognition of where our true deliverance lies. Amen.

12

The Vineyard

"Let me now sing for by beloved a love song . . ."

ISAIAH 5:1A (RSV)

REAL MEN DON'T WEAR deodorant. So claimed Callum, a pungent civil servant from the Isle of Man. Whether or not his co-workers would have confirmed his claim we never discovered. But put Callum in a British pub with a Welshman and an Irishman arguing over several pints of beer as to which ethnic heritage held the best folk songs, and the olfactory offenses were soon transcended. In a mesmerizing melodic flow the songs poured out, songs of longing, songs of love, songs of sea and field, earthy songs with raucous choruses for all to join in. Love songs, of course, were the most poignant, most often mourning love lost.

> Let me now sing for my beloved a love song concerning his vineyard:
> My beloved had a vineyard on a very fertile hill.
> He digged it and cleared it of stones,
> and planted it with choice vines;
> he built a watchtower in the midst of it,
> and hewed out a wine vat in it . . .
> Isaiah 5:1–2a (RSV)

In Isaiah's world vineyards were everywhere. They must have been in order to support the level of wine consumption and inebriation described by Isaiah in this chapter. As Isaiah's listeners already knew, vine and vineyard were traditional symbols for Israel, God's people. Even Jesus used vineyard imagery in various parables as well as in describing himself as the vine, his Father as the vinedresser, and his followers as branches (John 15).

In the sixteenth century Lucas Cranach the Younger created a popular painting called "The Vineyard of the Lord" to represent the Christian church as God's vineyard, rich with allegorical references to Protestant and Catholic contrasts. Not unlike Isaiah, parts of Cranach's artistic metaphor illustrate a vineyard in disarray where human agendas have supplanted God's.

For Isaiah, the love story of the vineyard was a "hook," a surefire device for getting his listeners' attention. He tricks them into thinking that they are to judge someone else's transgressions, when in fact he is setting them up to judge their own.

> And now, inhabitants of Jerusalem and people of Judah,
> judge between me and my vineyard.
> What more was there to do for my vineyard that I have not done in it?
> When I expected it to yield grapes, why did it yield wild grapes?
> Isaiah 5:3–4 (NRSV)

The prophet Nathan pulled the same trick on the adulterous King David with a story about a rich man who stole a poor man's prized lamb. When King David condemned the deed, Nathan uttered the convicting words: "You are the man," to which David responded, "I have sinned against the Lord." (2 Samuel 12, RSV)

Unfortunately, Isaiah's audience did not respond with equal candor, though it was not for lack of effort on Isaiah's part.

> For the vineyard of the Lord of hosts is the house of Israel,
> and the people of Judah are his pleasant planting;
> he expected justice, but saw bloodshed;
> righteousness, but heard a cry! . . .
> And now I will tell you what I will do to my vineyard.
> I will remove its hedge, and it shall be devoured;
> I will break down its wall, and it shall be trampled down.
> I will make it a waste; it shall not be pruned or hoed,
> and it shall be overgrown with briers and thorns;
> I will also command the clouds that they rain no rain upon it.
> Isaiah 5:7, 5–6 (NRSV)

Was God's reaction vindictive? To manipulate nature itself in punishment—though commonly thought to occur in the Old Testament point of view—seems a little extreme, especially when the parable heralds such love. Isaiah's description of Judah as God's "pleasant planting" reveals genuine affection for the beloved, an expectation of harmony and pleasure in the relationship. One is reminded of Eden, the Genesis account of how God created something very good but then found it corrupted, trust betrayed. There, too, the consequences were harsh. The "vineyard" was lost, the inhabitants exiled. In similar ways both Isaiah and Genesis describe a broken relationship, but one which is based on an initially loving connection.

To accept that assumption, though, is to be faced with the question that has plagued believers ever since such belief began, namely "How can God be both loving and judgmental?" Does unrequited love justify such utter destruction? ("I will break down its wall, and it shall be trampled down.") Jilted lovers can be vengeful. The animosity evident in so many nasty divorces attests to that sad reality. But is this what we want to see in God?

For Isaiah, the crux of the matter hinged on justice. God was simply exercising the terms of the covenant as originally established: "and he looked for justice, but behold, bloodshed; for righteousness, but behold, a cry!"

In Scripture the biblical concept of justice can be seen evolving over time to mean everything from simply what is "straight" and "true" in a physical sense to rules that should guide judges in making decisions, from simple fair play in human interaction to the moral standards by which God judges human deeds, from punishment for sin to the act of pity, love, and grace by which God "imputes" or bestows righteousness on us fallible mortals. God's "just-ification" is God's looking at us through the eyes of love rather than judgment, focusing on our worthiness instead of our failures and flaws.

When Isaiah speaks of justice he expresses particular concern with the way people treat each other and with the way their life together reflects and honors God. The threats and punishments described by Isaiah are first of all intended to "scare" people back to just behavior, but do at the same time serve notice as to the inevitable consequences of their errant ways.

In verse 23 Isaiah offers a specific example: "Woe to those who acquit the guilty for a bribe, and deprive the innocent of his right!" Clearly, in Isaiah's perspective justice is a relational, even individual matter. Thanks to Isaiah and others like him, most of us have this inner conviction that each and every person has a "right" to just treatment. This concept plays out still, whether as articulated in the American Constitution and Bill of Rights or in the United Nations Declaration of Human Rights. The absence of justice appalls human conscience and repeatedly motivates heroic acts of both defiance and advocacy on behalf of others. The Civil Rights movement of the 1960s and the global efforts of organizations such as Amnesty International or Human Rights Watch are contemporary examples.

Seen in that context—God's concern for healthy human community and the calling to account of abuses and injustice—perhaps the severity of God's warnings and action are not so extreme. Is there not a reassuring consistency in a God whose passion for humanity's well-being should find humanity's destructive behaviors so offensive, even to the point of meting out harsh penalties?

To emphasize his point Isaiah ends this parable of weal and woe with a description of the intimidating methodology God plans to employ. Isaiah pointedly contrasts the strength, invincibility, and perfection of the punishing foe with the weakness, brokenness, and disarray of Judah's situation:

> He will raise a signal for a nation far away,
> and whistle for a people at the ends of the earth;
> Here they come, swiftly, speedily!
> None of them is weary, none stumbles, none slumbers or sleeps,
> not a loincloth is loose, not a sandal-thong broken;
> their arrows are sharp, all their bows bent,
> their horses' hoofs seem like flint,
> and their wheels like the whirlwind.
> Isaiah 5:26–28 (NRSV)

But for Isaiah an even bigger point is in play here, namely, that God's sovereignty is universal. As an astute observer of the political milieu in which he lived, Isaiah knew that the Assyrian armies were eventually coming. But he implicitly understands them as one of the chosen actors in a greater cosmic drama. For the author of all human history, the application of justice extends beyond the confines of Judah to the entire human community. All nations have a part to play.

For Discussion

1. How would you define justice, and where did you get your definition? Are there universal concepts of justice?
2. How is justice manifested in your life—socially, politically, in the workplace, in your family, and in your relationships?

For Reflection

We have all experienced broken relationships. Some of life's deepest wounds come from the betrayals, failures, and harm done to us by those we love or by us to others, including those we love most. How has such pain damaged or soured the vineyard of your life? Where, after investing time, love, and effort have you looked for choice fruit and found instead wild, bitter grapes? If the harvest was one of anger or disappointment, did a harsh response resolve the pain, or does resentment remain? Where you sowed seeds of hope, did disappointment displace love? Were your expectations realistic? What were they based on? Love? Self-interest? How could you reclaim and restore the vineyard that is your life, rebuild the walls, replant choice vines? Isaiah's words are rich with the inspiring message that you, too, are God's pleasant planting—as well as with the corollary that others are too.

For Prayer

Vineyard-building God, we are your pleasant planting. Nourish us with love and hope. Prune us as needed to produce rich, choice fruit in our lives. Amen.

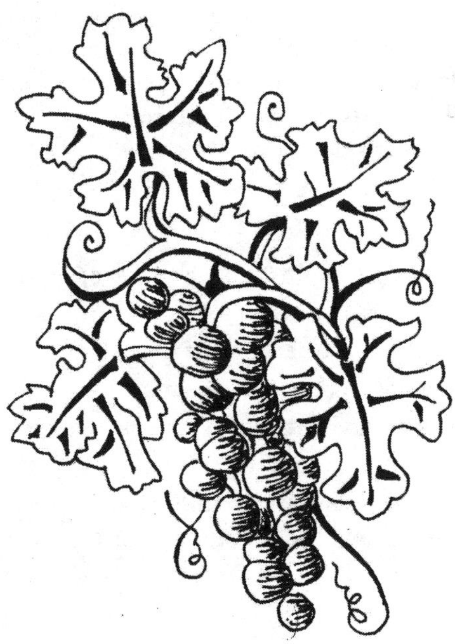

13

Woes

"People are bowed down, everyone is brought low,
and the eyes of the haughty are humbled.
But the LORD of hosts is exalted by justice,
and the Holy God shows himself holy by righteousness."

ISAIAH 5:15–16 (NRSV)

ISAIAH FOLLOWS HIS SONG of unrequited love with six "woes" describing what God's people have done wrong and how they are going to pay for it.

> Woe to those who join house to house, who add field to field,
> until there is no more room,
> and you are made to dwell alone in the midst of the land.
> The LORD of hosts has sworn in my hearing:
> "Surely many houses shall be desolate,
> large and beautiful houses, without inhabitant."
> Isaiah 5:8–9 (RSV)

Before the 2008–2010 housing market collapse in the United States, as many as one-third of all home sales were for people buying second homes as vacation or investment properties. The "have's" were "having more" by "joining house to house." More than 150 years before that, Midwestern farm land was divided into "sections," each a square mile. Sections were divided into "quarters" of 160 acres each. Those, in turn, were halved into eighty-acre plots and then often halved again—just enough to support a single family with crops and livestock.

Today almost no one can survive on so little land farming similar crops. Out of economic necessity farmers have had to "add field to field" until the average farm size in a state like Minnesota today is nearly 350 acres, four times the original norm. But if you drive the rural roads of many states you can still find the collapsed barns and dilapidated shells of homes where families once live and children played. Today instead of being able to walk to the neighboring farm house for help or a visit, farmers often have to drive for miles to meet a neighbor. In the 1980s and 1990s Minnesota alone is said to have lost as many as ten thousand family farms. No one needs to tell those still living in such rural areas what the ensuing population decline means to rural communities: jobs are lost, local businesses disappear, schools close, community cohesiveness and connections are eroded.

As Isaiah prophesied, when such expansion occurs, "you are made to dwell alone in the midst of the land." Of course, the aloneness Isaiah was talking about was the desolation that would come with exile—a land denuded by deportation and death. But the irony remains that when "field is added to field," whether driven by market forces or a desire to accumulate, one of the consequences is that the very community life that makes expansion desirable is diminished.

Isaiah also issues other woes related to excess. In particular he picks on the kind of self-absorbed, self-indulgent lifestyle that leads to a disregard for the One who is the true source of all pleasure and good and on those who treat their neighbors unjustly.

> Woe to those who rise early in the morning,
> that they may run after strong drink,
> who tarry late into the evening till wine inflames them!
> They have lyre and harp, timbrel and flute and wine at their feasts;
> but they do not regard the deeds of the Lord or see the work of his hands.
> Isaiah 5:11–12 (RSV)

> Woe to those who are heroes at drinking wine, and valiant men in mixing strong drink, who acquit the guilty for a bribe, and deprive the innocent of his right!
> Isaiah 5:22–23 (RSV)

Disregarding the fact that most people who "run after strong drink" are too hung over to rise early to drink more, it is nevertheless true that the wine market around the world has received abundant attention in recent years. Americans, while still far behind most countries in the Western hemisphere in per capita consumption (eight liters per person versus sixty or so in France and the Vatican City State), may soon surpass second-ranked Italy in wine consumption by volume (cases drunk). Wine-tastings, wine making, wine magazines, even wine investing, are more popular than ever. But that is not what Isaiah was talking about. His focus was the consequences of blindness, on putting self-indulgence ahead of communal conscience. Addiction, the ravages of a meth-addicted life, chemical abuse of all kinds—these are but examples not only of human fragility and broken community, but also of a severed connection between humanity and God, of a deeply flawed focus on that which destroys rather than that which gives life.

Isaiah utilizes a poignant phrase to express this damaged connection: "Therefore my people go into exile for want of knowledge" (Isaiah 5:13a, RSV). In Buddhism the first step on the Eightfold Path to Enlightenment is "Right Knowledge." To journey towards deliverance, one must begin with a proper understanding of reality. For Isaiah and the people of Judah, this meant having a clear recognition of their "reason for being." Namely, they were the children of the covenant God; their purpose was to serve and to witness to God's being with obedience, trust, and justice. The alternative was exile—physical, social, and even spiritual separation from God, from one another, and from the place which grounded their identity.

"Therefore Sheol has enlarged its appetite" (Isaiah 5:14a, RSV). In the Middle Ages and well into the sixteenth century "Doom paintings" were common on canvases, altar triptychs, and wall murals in rural English churches. At a time when few people could read, art and stained glass windows were a key tool for conveying biblical stories and church teachings. For a people familiar with the Black Death, the recurring and devastating plague which wiped out nearly a third of Europe's population, apocalyptic fears ran high. These fears were compounded by the invading armies of the great Suleiman the Magnificent whose Ottoman armies had marched across eastern Europe to the very gates of Vienna by 1529.

In a famous altar panel by the sixteenth century Dutch artist Lucas van Leyden entitled "The Last Judgment," hell is depicted as a great fish-like beast swallowing sinners into the rising flames of fiery, eternal torment.

> Therefore Sheol has enlarged its appetite
> and opened its mouth beyond measure;
> the nobility of Jerusalem and her multitude go down,
> her throng and all who exult in her.
> Isaiah 5:14 (NRSV)

Among those destined to go down to Sheol, the place of the dead, are the subjects of Isaiah's added "Woes:"

> Woe to those who draw iniquity with cords of falsehood,
> who draw sin as with cart ropes . . .
> Woe to those who call evil good and good evil,
> who put darkness for light and light for darkness,
> who put bitter for sweet and sweet for bitter!
> Woe to those who are wise in their own eyes,
> and shrewd in their own sight!
> Isaiah 5:18, 21–22 (RSV)

"Spin control" has become a staple of modern political life. Those with the greatest clout and media access can shape the public's perception of events to their advantage even if that includes "calling evil good and good evil." One of the greatest assets of the Nazi war machine in World War II—and a model for governments ever since—was its understanding of and ability to utilize propaganda on a mass scale. Some would argue that one of the great propaganda coups of American political campaigning was the "swift boat" spinning of the 2004 presidential election which saw a candidate's established war record shredded. Others would point to Hollywood political "docu-dramas" as the opposite side of the same coin. Either way, as Isaiah's prophecy indicates, God definitely plans to put a "spin" on all those who twist truth to manipulate others, all those "wise in their own eyes" who take unto themselves exploitative power over others, in effect putting themselves in the place of God.

With his woe pronouncements Isaiah confronted those who "would draw iniquity with cords of falsehood." That included those in his own religious community. There were no doubt those in Isaiah's circle who dismissed his depiction of what God was about to do. For, Isaiah, too, had his critics who thought they knew better than Isaiah what constituted God's will and who dismissed his judgmental pronouncements.

At the same time, we know that warnings of woe have always appealed to some portions of the faith community. In the Christian community ever since New Testament times, for example, there have always been those who passionately and often with disturbing delight have expounded impending doom. For believers today, however, there is a risk in focusing on judgment and woes. Whether expressed through medieval painting, "rapture fiction," or pulpit rants about God's Judgment Day, believers can be tempted to go too far towards wishful, holier-than-thou, even vengeful thinking which actually distorts the biblical message and misrepresents God's greater intent as presented in scripture as a whole. True, scripture is consistent in proclaiming that God has plans for judgment one day. But God's greater purpose was to steer people away from judgment towards redemption. In that sense, perhaps Isaiah's warnings of woe for his people in Judah should also serve as a caution to complacent and self-righteous believers of all kinds in the world today. For, in the end, the woes Isaiah proclaimed led to a tragic result for those accused:

> Therefore the anger of the Lord was kindled against his people,
> and he stretched out his hand against them and smote them, and
> the mountains quaked;
> and their corpses were as refuse in the midst of the streets.
> For all this his anger is not turned away and his hand
> is stretched out still.
> Isaiah 5:25 (RSV)

These could not have been comforting words to Isaiah's listeners. They are not comforting to us. Instead, they are a message of accountability and of the consequences for exploitative, corrupted, fruitless lives, both for individuals and for communities. The prophets excelled at such messages. That's partly why we have preserved their words. The warnings of the past apply equally to the present.

Comfort comes in recalling the broader context of Isaiah's Vineyard song, expressed in the opening line: "Let me sing for my beloved," reiterated in God's description of the vineyard as "his pleasant planting." As strained and as painful as the relationship can become and no matter how severe the consequences, the relationship continues. The people chastened are still recognized as God's people. God does destroy the vineyard, but not the beloved.

For Discussion

1. Does the comfortable, insulated life most of us lead diminish our capacity to grasp terror, to quake before life's apocalyptic possibilities? Are we oblivious to the "woes" that might justly afflict us someday?
2. Why do we resist judgment? Why do we find Isaiah's words so uncomfortable and perhaps even try to write them off as an archaic rant irrelevant to us today?

For Reflection

Our culture tells us to accumulate, to seek security through material means. Self-indulgence is encouraged. Global society, despite its setbacks and traumas, includes the promise of continual progress toward a "better world." How confident are you in such an outcome? How secure do you feel?

Heeding Isaiah's warnings, evaluate how liable you are to the "woes" he defines. Then locate an item in your immediate surroundings that gives you encouragement. It could be a religious symbol that signifies forgiveness, redemption, and hope. Or, it could be the view out your window of a tree or water that symbolizes the persistent, ever-renewing possibilities of life. Resolve to pursue a balance between the realistic awareness of justified woes and a hopeful openness to redemptive possibilities for all of us.

For Prayer

Sovereign God, in your mercy deliver us from destructive behaviors. Turn our hearts towards compassion, our minds towards truth, and our lives towards the joy and peace of living in harmony with you. Amen.

14

Angel Sex

"With two, he covered his feet"

ISAIAH 6:2 (RSV)

DO ANGELS HAVE SEX? Apparently they do. In both Genesis (6:2, 4) and Numbers (13:33) there are references to the Nephilim, a semi-mythological group of heavenly beings who mated with mortals. Whether or not that is historically true and whether or not they were angels as we think of them today, we know from Scripture that angels do indeed have gender. Isaiah, for example, saw male angels when he was first called to be a prophet (at least in the RSV translation of the original Hebrew):

> In the year that King Uzziah died
> I saw the Lord sitting upon a throne, high and
> lifted up; and his train filled the temple.
> Above him stood the seraphim: each had six wings:
> with two he covered his face, and with two, he covered his feet,
> and with two he flew.
> Isaiah 6:1–2 (RSV)

While there are over three hundred references to angels in Scripture, this is the only passage that mentions seraphim. Some scholars see Isaiah's seraphim as vision-enhanced versions of griffin-like creatures sometimes depicted in ancient Near Eastern art. Others speculate that the word seraphim derives from an association with fiery serpent-like creatures (such as mentioned in Numbers 21:6). How ironic then, that the seraph who touched Isaiah's lips had to use tongs to pick up the flaming ember, presumably in order not to get burned.

Another unique aspect of these seraphim is what they did with their wings. Some scholars maintain that the phrase "with two he covered his feet" is actually a euphemism for the angel covering his genitals. If that is true, what does it say about angels? That they are modest? Are they all male? Or is the male imagery simply a paternalistic projection from a patriarchal culture?

Does it matter? After all, angel gender is not the real issue in this text. What is most important about the seraphim is what they represent. Like angels elsewhere in Scripture, the seraphim are heralds of the divine. They communicate and enact God's will. Here the seraphim proclaimed God's holiness. But they also proclaimed God's glory on earth.

Why? What was the point of their noting that "the whole earth is full of his glory?" Was it merely a reinforcement of what Isaiah was experiencing in his vision, confirming that what he was perceiving were heavenly realities? Or were the angels affirming the connection between God and creation, the fact that this world we live in is touched by—even "full of"—the grace and glory of God?

The seraphim were verbal beings. That should not surprise us. This whole text is full of dialogue—angel to angel, angel to Isaiah, God to Isaiah, and Isaiah to God. As we have seen before, the biblical God is a speaking God, one who initiates and invites communication. Remarkably, God's first words in this account come in the form of a question, "Whom shall I send, and who will go for us?" This question echoes God's great question to Adam and Eve in the Garden of Eden (as well as to the rest of us), "Where are you?" (Genesis 3:9).

God's asking such questions suggests that multiple answers are possible. God's questions create space for us to choose a response. The God who asks questions is not a dictatorial god who gives us no options but is, rather, the God of free will.

It's as though God is here presented as the "Head of Human Resources" for the cosmos, recruiting talent for the divine business plan. God's asking, "Whom shall I send?" is like a political or military leader motivating potential recruits by challenging them to join a noble cause.

Particularly interesting in this invitation is the plural pronoun in God's question, "who will go for *us*?" Compare that with God's saying, "Let *us* make man in *our* image, after *our* likeness" at Creation (Genesis 1:26a, italics added). Who is this "us" God is referring to? Is it simply "the royal 'we,'" a mode of expression familiar to kings and queens speaking on behalf of their crown, their heritage, and their people? Is it a reference to the heavenly hosts as exemplified by the seraphim in this text? Could it even be a reference to the Trinity, as some suggest? Or, is it a reminder that God transcends our categories of comprehension, that God manifests a wholeness beyond our understanding, a trans-individuated existence, as it were, beyond singularity, gender, or physical identification?

However we understand this pronoun, the fact that there is a pronoun at all is what is important. For, pronouns are expressions of personhood and relationship, which is ultimately what this text is about: the relational God is reaching out to engage a human being in order to convey God's message to other human beings, not only in Isaiah's day, but also in ours, we could argue, by virtue of the continued existence of this text.

The seraphim certainly were key players in this drama. Throughout Scripture the heavenly host are presented as actively engaged in divine-human encounters. From Hagar to Jacob, from Gideon to Mary, from Balaam's ass to Peter, angels appear, sometimes with warnings and death, at other times bringing comfort, good news, and liberation. In modern times angels are often portrayed as cute figures or as quirky characters in Hollywood movies. In contrast to the fearsome, majestic, and powerful creatures depicted in Scripture, people today prefer their angels to be cuddly, almost as if they would make good pets. We have all seen angels turned into good luck charms, dashboard dolls, and shiny bracelet bangles.

Isaiah would never have recognized such creatures. After all, the one he encountered stuck a burning coal in his face. But what was truly important about that was the forgiveness mediated by the experience.

> "Woe is me! I am lost; for I am a man of unclean lips,
> and I live among a people of unclean lips . . ."
> Isaiah 6:5a (NRSV)

Isaiah recognized his unworthiness to stand in the presence of God. He realized his vulnerability as a flawed mortal confronted by divine reality. Isaiah grasped what we too often do not, namely, that there is a difference between us and God. Modern culture, on the other hand, too often amplifies the primal sin of the Garden of Eden, namely, the desire and the attempts by human beings to be as gods themselves. New age religions, including some new age versions of Christianity—not unlike the Gnosticism in Christianity's early centuries—seek to discover godhood within human beings, often revealed or attained by focusing exclusively on the self. Inevitably, this contributes to a smug sense of superiority over other, "less enlightened" or less "self-actualized" individuals. Modern materialism and the "culture of me" feed a similar self-divination. Money, status, and possessions become the measures of personal value. Life's focus becomes the self over the other, rather than one's neighbor or the supremely Other, God.

Isaiah understood the necessary difference between human being and God-being. He recognized that because he was at risk. He knew that mortals cannot play god and survive. Isaiah also understood that his whole community was at risk, deluded by their self-absorption. With trepidation he confessed the truth. But the angel touched him, saying, "Behold, this has touched your lips; your guilt is taken away and your sin forgiven." By heaven's grace Isaiah was freed from both fear and failure and made worthy to commune with the divine. Nothing he could have done on his own would have accomplished this. Via the angel's mediation God erased his culpability and opened the way for him to both be in God's presence and to do God's work even as the angel had done.

Isaiah could not have expected what followed—as if anything about this extraordinary experience was predictable! God's conversation inaugurated a call that would fill the rest of Isaiah's life with purpose, passion, and profound frustration. This encounter with heavenly possibilities birthed a complex message of judgment and hope that would shape humanity's future for centuries to come.

One wonders what the seraphim thought about that . . . and what they're up to now.

For Discussion

1. What do you think about angels? Do they exist? (Polls have showed that two-thirds of Americans think they do.) Have you encountered any?
2. Angels told Mary, then Joseph, then the shepherds (among others) to "Be not afraid." But in the Old Testament and in the New Testament book of Revelation, angels are often terrifying. Do we need to

experience both fear and comfort for spiritual growth?

3. Forgiveness for Isaiah was mediated by a six-winged seraph. How is forgiveness mediated and pronounced to you? How, in turn, can you mediate and pronounce the liberating power of sin forgiven and guilt removed to others?

For Reflection

Isaiah was at the right place at the right time to receive God's contact because he had joined himself to the religious practices of his community. He was at worship. He was in community. He practiced his faith. None of that guaranteed that he would receive the vision and the call he did. But would he have received it otherwise? Consider how the choices you make in terms of personal spiritual practices might contribute to perceiving God's presence and calling in your own life. Recall that the angel touched Isaiah in the mouth, preparing Isaiah to speak for God. Where do you need to be touched to better become God's instrument?

For Prayer

Touch us, God, with the embers of deliverance. Incinerate our guilt that we may be purified and prepared for fuller communion with you. Fire our imagination with glimpses of heavenly glory that we may better perceive the fullness of your glory in the world around us. Amen.

15

Axial Moments

"In the year that King Uzziah died . . ."

ISAIAH 6:1A (RSV)

MORE PERHAPS THAN WE acknowledge, death defines us. Many Baby Boomers still remember where they were when President John F. Kennedy was shot. For almost as many, the assassination of Martin Luther King marked an equally defining moment. The 9/11 attacks, hurricane Katrina—such deadly events have been seared into the public memory.

Privately, death holds equal sway. "The year my mother died," "the year our son was killed in Iraq," "the year our daughter was abducted"—life is never the same again after death touches us, even if it does not always come in such violent or dramatic ways.

The call of Isaiah was set in the framework of a significant death. During Uzziah's long reign, the people of Judah enjoyed their last great period of national prominence, pride, and prosperity. But the tides of history were shifting. Following Uzziah's passing, the Israelite nation entered a pattern of alternating decline and recovery, leading to its ultimate disappearance altogether as an independent political state for more than two thousand years.

Many of us today can relate. Whether it is through draining international military conflicts or market chaos in the global economic system, history repeats itself. Into exactly such a context God called Isaiah and sent him to decry the corruption and bad political choices which led to such a fall but also to proclaim the hope that beyond the impending darkness a new chapter would begin.

Given the historical sea-change that occurred in Isaiah's lifetime, Isaiah's call can be seen as marking an "axial moment" in history. Axial moments are those that represent a turning point, a period of history when events and personalities converge in such a way as to impact all that follows. The rise of the Roman Empire can be seen as one such axial moment. The coalescing of power under first Julius and then Augustus Caesar between roughly 50 BCE and 15 CE began the reordering of the Mediterranean world, redefining the political structure of Europe for the next one thousand years, and impacting the languages, laws, and economics of cultures from the Middle East to the British Isles.

Within the context of *Pax Romana* an even more axial event took place, namely, the birth of Christianity. All the necessary pieces for the spread of Christian faith were conveniently in place: political stability, a relatively secure international travel system, an international currency, two "universal" languages (Latin and Greek), a diaspora community of Jews who could receive and support Jewish Christian evangelists, widely understood Greek philosophical concepts that could mediate Christian teaching, a highly developed literary culture with a portable literary medium (parchment and papyrus scrolls), and more. This moment was what later New Testament writers referred to as part of "the fullness of time" (Ephesians 1:10) and "when the time had fully come" (Galatians 4:4).

Another such axial moment occurred fifteen centuries later, when Europe began to shrug off the constraints of feudal society, the Black Death, and religious oppression. The genesis of modern capitalism, the foundations of contemporary nation states, the momentum of the Enlightenment, and the rise of modern science are all prefigured in the stunning fact that all of the following extraordinary individuals were alive at exactly the same moment in human history: Martin Luther, Leonardo da Vinci, Christopher Columbus, King Henry VIII, Suleiman the Magnificent, Nicolaus Copernicus, Michaelangelo, Jacob Fugger of the Fugger banking family, Desiderius Erasmus, the Aztec ruler Montezuma II, Ferdinand Magellan, Hernando Cortez, John Calvin, Jesuit founder Ignatius Loyola, Niccolo Machiavelli, Philip Melancthon, Albrecht Dürer, William Tyndale, Ponce de Leon, Pope Leo X, Thomas Cranmer, Thomas More, Ulrich Zwingli, Francis Xavier, Emporer Charles V, John Knox, and Ivan III the Great, the "Lord of all the Russias," to name a few.

Identifying axial moments is naturally a subjective exercise. One might make an equal case for the century following the birth of the prophet Mohammed in the Arab world, or the roughly two-hundred-year span from 500 to 300 BCE that gave us Confucius, Lao Tzu, the prophet Jeremiah, the Buddha, and Alexander the Great.

Many might agree that the world today is experiencing a profound axial moment, given the extraordinary coalescence of technological advances in the last century, including everything from air travel to moon landings, from television to computers, from Gatling guns and mustard gas to nuclear arsenals and bio-weapons. Included in just the last one hundred years are such influential history changing figures as Albert Einstein, Mao Tse Tung, Winston Churchill, Franklin D. Roosevelt, Mahatma Ghandi, Mother Theresa, Martin Luther King, Pope John Paul II, and too many other distinguished scientists, artists, and leaders to mention.

The tides of national histories are shifting again in this global age even more dramatically than they did in Isaiah's day. But Isaiah's message carries through even to modern times, perhaps becoming more relevant than ever. Isaiah's call to accountability and social justice resonates in cultures from North America to the Middle East, from Central America to East Asia. Isaiah's inspiring imagery of the wolf dwelling with the lamb, of swords being beat into plowshares (Isaiah 11:6, 2:4), is more than an appealing ideal in a world facing profound cultural conflicts, devastating levels of violence, and the possibility of nuclear or climatic extinction. It may be a critical image for the very survival of the human race. It may help prevent death from defining human history itself.

For Discussion

1. What "defining deaths" have you experienced? Whose passing has most affected or stuck with you? Why?
2. Do you agree with the concept of "axial moments" in history, times when the coalescence of events and individuals impacts all that follows, changing human history forever? If so, would you say we are living in such a time? Identify what might make that case.

For Reflection

In the streaming tides of human history where do you fit? Would you describe yourself more as a speck of matter floating on the stream of life or as a protruding stone affecting the flow of the stream? How does one find significance in history's grand flow? Does one need to?

Imagine yourself being carried in the current along with all human beings who have ever lived or ever will. Feel the comfort of company. Recognize and accept the uncertainties of never seeing the whole stream or where it ends. Celebrate the motion and energy of both the steady and the swirling currents. Relish the white-water sprays, the rock-shaping power, the deep, still calm. Marvel at all the life engendered within the watery marvel of the river of being.

For Prayer

Lord of life, death, and destiny, we yield ourselves to your cosmic currents. We honor with gratitude the rich contributions of people both past and present in cultures everywhere to the unfolding of human history. We trust ourselves to the future, confident that death does not finally define anything. Amen.

16

Seeing God

"I saw the LORD sitting upon a throne, high and lifted up;
and his train filled the temple."

ISAIAH 6:1B (RSV)

WHAT DO THE PYRAMID of Giza, the Parthenon, Notre Dame Cathedral and the United Nations building in New York all have in common? According to those who perceive it in both art and nature, there is a fundamental mathematical calculation called "Phi" which can be discovered not only in the structures already mentioned but in the art of Leonardo da Vinci, the mathematical formulas of Euclid and Pythagoras, and in many of Europe's great cathedrals, including those in Rheims, France and Milan, Italy. Also called the Golden Ratio, the Golden Mean or Section, and the Divine Proportion, this organizing principle of physical form is said to be discernable organically as well, in everything from the human body to snail shells. Da Vinci's famous "Vitruvian Man," the drawing of a figure, arms and legs spread wide, inside both a square and a circle, illustrates the popular Renaissance idea that set proportions permeated the whole of nature, art, and architecture.

Does heaven have Phi? Does Isaiah's vision offer us any clues to a divinely proportioned cosmic order? Clearly, Isaiah's vision had a spatial dimension, with God seen as "high and lifted up" with the seraphim visible "above him" (Isaiah 6:2a) and with God's "train," or royal robes filling the temple. In addition Isaiah recounted how "the foundations of the thresholds shook" in response to sound waves ("the voice of him who called") which suggests a solidity to the divine realm. However, it should also be duly noted that shaking foundations were a typical image widely used in Scripture to describe divine theophanies, or the experiences of God's overwhelming, physically eventful appearances.

For Isaiah the whole visionary experience was an intensely sensory one. It was visual ("I saw"), auditory (the angels spoke, God spoke, Isaiah spoke), tactile (touched in the mouth), perhaps even olfactory ("and the house was filled with smoke"). What does all this tell us, not just about Isaiah's experience, but about how humans see God?

In Old Testament terms Isaiah's experience was hardly unique. Abraham experienced God's presence in a mysterious encounter involving animal carcasses, deep darkness, and a smoking fire pot (Genesis 15). Jacob had the ladder dream with its obvious vertical dimension (Genesis 28:10–17). Elijah encountered God in a mountainside experience dramatized by violent wind, earthquake, fire, and finally, the still small voice (1 Kings 19:9). Moses and those involved in the exodus from Egypt witnessed God's presence repeatedly in smoke, fire, cloud, and quaking earth, not to mention the ten plagues. Ezekiel's vision of heaven was not unlike Isaiah's in that it featured winged beings bearing burning coals, a high throne, the voice of God, wind, fire, and other manifestations of the heavenly realm ("The heavens were opened, and I saw visions of God"—Ezekiel 1b). Not until the book of Revelation at the end of the New Testament do we find a more Phi-like presentation of the heavenly realm in the neatly measured and richly decorated layout of the new Jerusalem which comes to crown a new heaven and a new earth (Revelation 21).

The Greek philosopher Plato argued that the world as we know it is modeled after an ideal version of reality. More recent thinkers in the field of psychology have maintained that our images of the world beyond—or the very concept that a world "beyond" even exists—are merely projections from our human experiences, fears, desire—and brain chemistry. Those who study epistemology, or how we learn and know things, might see language itself as the progenitor of our perceptions, divine or otherwise. Or, one can merely hold to the simple conviction that there is a harmonic reality to all existence, heavenly as well as earthly, which resonates in parallel in whatever realm.

Stephen Hawking, the famous wheel-chair-bound physicist, was once asked if he believed in God. He responded that he believed in the laws of physics universally applied, which ruled out the possibilities of miracles and therefore God. Then he added in his unique, computer-generated cadence that those who believe in an afterlife are simply people who are afraid of the dark.

In contrast, Sir John T. Houghton, an Oxford physicist and colleague of Hawking, has argued that one can understand the concept of God and heaven via physics itself, particularly "string theory," which raises the possibility of additional dimensions to the ones we already know (space and time). God and the things of heaven may be simply a "Fifth Dimension" able to penetrate ours.

Sir Martin Rees, another distinguished British astronomer and physicist, has noted that not only may multiple dimensions exist and be able to interact with ours, but they may have different physical laws than the ones which operate in our space and time continuum. If that were the case, the laws of nature which Hawking and others use to rule out God could no longer serve that purpose.

Whether as a matter of physics, psychology, or religious reality, human beings will inevitably perceive and describe the divine in terms of what they already know. Our history and experiences are the only conceptual parameters we have available to us. God, on the other hand, can by definition exceed all our parameters, even to the point of creating new realities altogether, for example, Resurrection.

Isaiah's encounter with God is not entirely unfathomable. His vision occurred in the temple at Jerusalem. Biblical descriptions, historical records, and archaeological evidence have established the existence, nature, and religious practices of that particular temple. We know that Isaiah's vision closely correlated with the physical environment in which he was worshiping. The temple had an altar and burning embers. So did his vision. Both had a threshold, a point of crossing over from the ordinary world into holy space. Smoke from the altar and perhaps from incense as well filled both the physical and visionary atmospheres. There were throne images in each: the likely elevated platform of the Ark of the Covenant, symbol of God's presence in the Jerusalem temple, and the elevated throne of God personally present in Isaiah's vision. Isaiah saw angels. In the Jerusalem temple there were images of winged cherubim embossed on the gold-covered walls of the inner sanctuary. Both Isaiah's social reality and his spiritual reality included kings. Isaiah's prophecy opens with reference to the death of Judah's King Uzziah. In his temple vision Isaiah states "my eyes have seen the king," this time referring to the king of all creation. This vision may even have taken place during a Hebrew festival marking the supreme kingship of God over Israel.

Do the evident parallels somehow diminish Isaiah's vision? Or do the points of connection between heaven and earth in Isaiah's vision convey a reassuring sense of continuity between divine reality and human reality? If we can identify the potentially causative roots of Isaiah's vision, does that somehow make it less valid? If an experience of God is less than completely "supernatural," is it therefore untrue? In either case, the marvel and mystery of Isaiah's vision will never diminish. Nor will the marvel and mystery of how any of us envision God.

For Discussion

1. Where do your images of heaven come from?
2. What would you like heaven to be? Would you like it to be interactive, so you could communicate with others? Or, is it all about flying around like the seraphim, singing praises to God?

For Reflection

Put yourself in Isaiah's place. Feel the fear, the awe, and the relief at being accepted and made pure. Imagine yourself standing in the divine presence, enveloped in an atmosphere of majesty and praise, with magnificent, winged angels hovering nearby. The voice of God addresses you directly. What does it say? What do you feel? Fear? Unworthiness? Joy? Yield yourself to the vision. Isaiah's fear was transformed by grace. Imagine yourself freed by that same grace. Then let the voice of God direct you as you return to your life's work.

For Prayer

God of transforming visions, open our eyes to heavenly realities in the midst of our earthly pursuits. By the hands of angels, winged or human, touch us with your grace so that we may be free to stand in your regal presence and hear your guiding voice. Amen.

17

Holy, Holy, Holy

"And one called to another and said:
'Holy, holy, holy is the Lord of hosts . . .'"

ISAIAH 6:3 (RSV)

Nearly twenty of us bundled into the back of a canvas-covered, Army surplus truck, excited about going to Bethlehem for Christmas Eve. The trip was a spur-of-the-moment excursion organized for volunteers at the kibbutz where we worked. Along the way, we stopped in Jerusalem, pulling over onto a graveled parking lot and piling out of the truck into a chilly wind and the unexpected sight of swirling snow settling onto whitening tufts of grass. Still, the flood-lit, stone-block towers and walls of the Old City glowed with an ethereal warmth against the darkening sky. Winding through the twisting stone streets, past hole-in-the-wall shops lit by hanging strings of light bulbs, we were warmed by anticipation of our first glimpse of the Western Wall, a site holy to Jews everywhere.

When we reached the sacred space before the ancient foundation stones of Herod's Temple Mount, we paused in respectful silence as black-clad rabbinic students swayed back and forth in devout recitations, prayer books in hand, while Israeli soldiers slung their weapons out of the way and tucked prayer slips between the great stone blocks. As first-time, non-Jewish visitors, some of us refrained from touching the sacred stones out of a presumed sense of reverence.

After a brief stay, it was time for the second leg of our holy night's journey to one of the most sacred sites for Christian faith: Bethlehem. We returned to the trucks, jostling together on the narrow bench seats for the short ride, not realizing that it would take us past military checkpoints, tanks, and Uzi-armed soldiers in increasing numbers as we neared the village. Just three years after the war which brought the Israeli army into Jerusalem and the West Bank, the birthplace of the Prince of Peace now lay encircled by the panoply of war.

In Manger Square choirs from Texas sang holiday hymns on trucked-in risers while Arab merchants hawked tacky Christmas trinkets to busloads of Finnish and Philippine pilgrims. The midnight mass, broadcast live, was projected in blurry images onto the outside wall of a nearby building. Overlooking the stone screen from the roof of the building Israeli soldiers perched with machine guns trained on the crowds below.

A little after two o'clock in the morning, the Mass ended and the shivering throngs from Manger Square crouched low through the famed Crusader entrance to the Church of the Nativity and entered the grotto below. In single file we edged down the steps to a low cove in the wall where a silver star inlaid on the rock and lit by multiple ornate lanterns marked the spot where Jesus was supposedly born. Reactions varied, from the pious tears of the spiritually moved to the skeptical curiosity of religious voyeurs—a fitting mortal parade past the mystery of the manger. At the end of the grotto, steps led up to the incense-laden sanctuary where we emerged to turn and see the words *Gloria in Excelsis Deo* emblazoned in an arc of red neon lights over the altar.

At that moment Christmas died. The incongruous combination of guns, crass tourism, and neon piety stripped Bethlehem of any remnant of holiness for all except those viewing it through a spiritually transcendent lens. The chilly ride home, as we huddled together for warmth in the open-backed truck rumbling into the pale dawn of another Christmas day, seemed a fitting end to the hollow holiness of Bethlehem on that particular Christmas Eve.

> And one called to another and said:
> "Holy, holy, holy is the LORD of hosts;
> the whole earth is full of his glory."
> And the foundations of the thresholds shook
> at the voice of him who called.
> Isaiah 6:3–4a (RSV)

Isaiah's experience in the temple in Jerusalem contrasted starkly with our Christmas Eve visit to Bethlehem. For, while we had gone seeking an artificial brush with the holy in an exotic location, the truly holy had come to him in the course of a regular religious routine. Like Moses drawn by God's angel to the burning bush centuries earlier (Exodus 3:2–5), Isaiah immediately recognized that he had traversed holy ground. The presence of angels, the voice of God, and the heavenly special effects all made that abundantly clear. But what did it all mean? What did Isaiah's experience do for him and why did he tell others about it?

The answer to the latter question is easy. Whether he shared his experience with others right away or waited until enough time had passed to process it, he ultimately understood the event as the defining moment of his life. It was the point of origin for his subsequent identity and purpose. His life was permanently changed—not always for the better—once the holy had penetrated his consciousness.

On a public level Isaiah's vision story confirmed his legitimacy as a prophet. It was his *curriculum vitae*, his ordination, the basis of his claim to authority. Although not disclosed in Scripture until the sixth chapter of the Old Testament book which bears his name, this experience was undoubtedly the opening announcement of his arrival as a messenger of God. Ironically, Isaiah's transcendent vision actually served a thoroughly pragmatic purpose. It became his ticket to the unholy. For, from this moment on, he would serve in the realm of political turmoil, social corruption, and religious opposition.

On a fundamental level, as happened for Isaiah, such an encounter with the holy understandably affects our perceptions of self and reality. Whether we experience holiness in the grandeur of nature, the moving harmonies of a symphony or of a beloved hymn, or in the embrace of another human being, holiness transforms us. In Isaiah's case it led him immediately to a concern for his community, those who he called "a people of unclean lips."

However it comes, the holy has the power to shape and redirect us, to change our priorities and relationships, to either turn us deeper into our own spiritual journey or to drive us out into the world for the sake of others, or both. The Buddha, following his enlightenment, chose out of compassion to share his discovery with others. Jesus, after his resurrection, returned to his disciples both to reassure them and to send them out to share the Good News with others. Isaiah went on from the temple experience to call kings and commoners alike to changed hearts and to an altogether new possibility for the future.

These examples suggest that holiness leads to more than abstract euphoria or spiritual self-indulgence. By nature, the holy draws us out of our placid assumptions and points us to greater realities, even to what many have described as an awareness of the ultimate Other, that which is utterly different from our fallible human selves, whether discerned as the Buddha reality or the God of Israel.

But holiness, though it transcends the mundane, does not reside in the trappings of the exceptional event, even if they include smoke or angels or flower petals falling from the Bodhi tree. Nor is holiness contained by rituals, emotions, by whatever we "set apart" to represent it, or even by the frightened awe it can engender. Holiness, in the end, is a matter of presence, not place or thing. Holiness is rooted in a connection, not a divide. If that were not true, the holy would be an empty, unfruitful phenomenon instead of a life-altering experience. Indeed, the hope of the holy is that it will change us, that it will fill us with inspiration based on the assurance that life has value and purpose, even as it did for Isaiah.

For Discussion

1. What does holiness mean to you? Have you experienced it in a way that you can recount or describe?
2. We all have stereotypes of the holy. Do they sometimes need to be shattered or at least challenged so that we do not confuse holiness with magic, for example, in assigning religious power to inanimate objects?

For Reflection

The New Testament holds an intriguing array of thought-provoking verses regarding holiness:

> "But as he who called you is holy, be holy yourselves . . ."
> (1 Peter 1:15, RSV)

> "But you are a chosen race, a royal priesthood, a holy nation, God's own people." (1 Peter 2:9a, RSV)

> "Put on then, as God's chosen ones, holy and beloved, compassion, kindness, lowliness, weakness, and patience . . ."
> (Colossians 3:12, RSV)

Holiness, these verses suggest, is a capacity within all of us. Consider your own holiness. Reflect on how you express it in the way you see and treat others. Under the dross we all accumulate—the failures, disappointments, imperfections, and pain—seek to discover what is holy about you, as well as in those around you. Let that be a guiding vision.

For Prayer

Holy God, imbue us with a sense of the holy. Attune us to the presence of your holiness in creation, in daily life, and in the people and world around us. May experiencing the holy not only nourish us spiritually but propel us into engagements with others which magnify holiness everywhere. Amen.

18

Send Me

"And I heard the voice of the LORD saying,
'Whom shall I send, and who will go for us?'
Then I said, 'Here am I! Send me.'"

ISAIAH 6:8 (RSV)

HOW MANY MISSIONARIES OVER the centuries have been inspired to their calling by these words? How many young people, sitting around campfires at religious retreats have been challenged to answer as Isaiah did? How many preachers have cajoled their listeners to take these words to heart in service, commitment, and giving to their congregations?

The call to personal commitment is compelling, perhaps even more so for religious purposes than for military service or public causes. Suicide bombers seeking heaven are a tragic example. A sense of purpose, a higher calling seems to be one of the deepest desires of the human spirit.

What was so utterly extraordinary about God's call to Isaiah, however, is that apparently Isaiah could have refused it just by keeping his mouth shut. For God's call came in the form of an open-ended question, almost a plea, "Who will go for us?" What kind of God does that, gives a mortal a choice? Does not divinity by definition mean the power to determine the outcome?

It is interesting to speculate what might have happened if Isaiah had responded to God's "Whom shall I send?" query differently, for example, "Anybody but me!" or "I don't know, God. Good luck with that!" One can imagine a Monty Python-type skit where Isaiah, Moses, or even Jesus in the Garden of Gethsemane chooses to refuse the call, thus changing the entire course of human history.

The truth is, human history is written largely around those who said, "Yes,"—often to invitations which, on the face of it, defied rational comprehension. People with as many faults and doubts as the rest of us agreed to undertakings the outcomes of which were totally beyond their imagining. Their saying "Yes" paved the way for possibilities that enriched countless others and altered global events.

Repeatedly, Scripture presents examples of this God who invites—sometimes even lures—people into a position where they are presented with a choice between alternatives. Adam and Eve in the Garden, Moses at the burning bush, Isaiah in the temple, Joshua addressing the Israelites ("Choose this day whom you will serve"—Joshua 24:15), Peter in the streets of Jerusalem at Pentecost (Acts 2), or Paul before the Athenians (Acts 17:16, 34)—all these represent a divine pattern of possibilities. This "possibility pattern" is strikingly consistent with a God who is continuously creative, a God who fills life with so many possibilities. Such a God is not a god who reigns as master over slave. Rather, the God who asks, "Where are you?" and "Who will go for us?" is one who demonstrates a remarkable degree of respect for the fallible mortals who have such a sad history of making bad choices.

Perhaps this sad history helps to explain the paradox which immediately follows Isaiah's call. For, after presenting Isaiah with a remarkable choice, God announces to Isaiah that choice is exactly what may be taken away from the people to whom Isaiah is sent.

> And he said, "Go, and say to this people:
> 'Hear and hear, but do not understand; see and see,
> but do not perceive.'
> Make the heart of this people fat, and their ears heavy,
> and shut their eyes;
> lest they see with their eyes, and hear with their ears,
> and understand with their hearts, and turn and be healed."
> Isaiah 6:9–10 (RSV)

That God on the one hand establishes a pattern of possibilities and honors the human capacity for making choices and then on the other hand threatens to deprive them of any capacity for understanding or responding seems to be a complete contradiction. Why would God commission a prophet to tell people that they would not understand what God was telling them and then would be punished for it?

Here lies the great irony of Isaiah's great call. He was to deliver a message that would inevitably be rejected. From the beginning he knew that his mission would to some degree be futile, and, clearly, it bothered him. So Isaiah asked,

> "How long, O Lord?"
> And he said: "Until cities lie waste without inhabitant,
> and houses without people, and the land is utterly desolate;
> and the LORD sends everyone far away,
> and vast is the emptiness in the midst of the land."
> Isaiah 6:11–12 (NRSV)

In the face of such a discouraging commission Isaiah's assent was remarkable. How are we to understand this paradox? It is the age-old question. How can a good God let bad things happen? Why would a God who goes to such efforts to communicate with us make it so hard to understand the divine plan?

Several responses emerge. In Isaiah's case, the good news is that God is speaking in the first place, sending someone to address these people, continuing a caring relationship. Secondly, there is the implied option of a positive outcome: "Otherwise they might see . . . hear . . . understand . . . turn and be healed." Healing is a response that God sees as possible. The inverted approach to it is almost like that of a frustrated parent who addresses a child's bad behavior with sarcasm, trying to intimidate or induce an outcome by threatening the opposite. But would the threat be made and the healing be mentioned if it were not already the preferred option?

Another aspect of this dilemma is free will. If God is a choice-giving God and if human beings are given a fair choice, does that not suggest that we can exercise good judgment and make appropriate choices without God resorting to such harsh threats?

Martin Luther, with his usual knack for presenting theological points in pithy terms, once said that, as far as free will is concerned, humans have just enough to milk a cow. By that he meant that free will has its limits. Like St. Augustine (to whose monastic religious order Luther once belonged) Luther believed that human free will is tainted by our fallen nature, by our inherent fallibility or "Original Sin." We humans do not have a god-like ability to make perfect choices. We inevitably lean towards self-serving, short-sighted decisions (which has interesting implications for everything from American individualism to political choices to investing to self-help trends). Ultimately, human free will works only as well as our responsiveness to divine guidance.

There is yet another way of looking at Isaiah's predicament in terms of dealing with the message he was given. In several places in the Old Testament most notably in the Exodus story, God "hardens the heart" of human beings, for example, Pharaoh and the Egyptians. The original Hebrew text for this passage in Isaiah says, "make the heart of this people 'fat.'" Today we know that fat clinging to the cardiac arteries as plaque can literally harden the heart. It is intriguing that the Hebrews used this image centuries ago to express a hardening of attitudes or human will as well.

God's hardening presumably enables a change in course, an outcome different than what would otherwise occur. It is as though God sometimes places a dam in the stream of human spiritual and political history so as to alter the flow of events and even to irrigate other fields. If Isaiah's message conveys another example of God "hardening the hearts" of God's people, then the question immediately arises as to the intent of that action.

On the one hand, one could argue that the hardening of one's heart—or of a nation's heart for that matter—is simply the inevitable result of making persistently bad choices, the natural consequence of bad habits, narrow-minded rigidity, clinging to power, ignoring advice, refusing to accept a broader view of reality. Spiritually put, the impact of persistent disobedience is a loss of perception, an inability to discern a saving way forward.

A sad manifestation of such hardening of the heart is familiar in interpersonal relationships. Who hasn't heard of friends or even siblings who, despite years of shared experiences and good memories, become alienated, vested in what divides them, and resistant to reconciliation? In marital breakdowns the moment seems to inevitably come when one spouse looks at the other with heart-hardened hostility, at some level choosing to discard or deny the love and the good that once was there and to close the door to its future return and the renewal of the relationship.

In that context Isaiah's call reflects one of the most remarkable themes in Hebrew Scripture, namely, the idea that God's election of a chosen people is designed to accomplish a far greater goal. Adam and Eve, the first couple, offer the first clue. Their presentation in the Bible precedes the covenant with Abraham which marked the setting apart of a particular covenant people. In the context of the creation story Adam and Eve are prototypes for the entire human race. Likewise, Noah, when he appears on the scene, represents humanity as a whole, a new Adam with whom God makes a covenant for all people. Even when the covenant with Abraham was established, it was explicitly a covenant designed to lead to the blessing of all earth's people ("By you all the families of the earth will be blessed"—Genesis 12:3). Isaiah and later prophets picked up that theme in various ways, referring to God's relationship with all of humanity and nature, even prophesying a day when all creatures will be united in a harmonious whole (e.g., Isaiah 11:6–9).

This almost "latent universalism" in Hebrew thought was extraordinary in the religious context of Israel's time. But its implication for believers today is just as profound. For it means that God's people can never claim utter exclusivity or superiority over others. Neither Christians nor Jews, for example, can have an absolute claim to divine favor. Whether understood in terms of Old Testament figures or the Gentiles of Christianity's early years, the work of God can be discerned as transcending all religious assumptions. Accordingly, if the God of all history deems it necessary for a whole nation—or religious tradition—to be consigned to blindness, misunderstanding, or its own errant ways—all for the sake of God's greater plan for humanity as a whole, then so be it. That is not only God's right; it is God's self-proclaimed intent.

Whether that strikes the believer as good news or bad probably depends on one's willingness to accept the paradigm. Isaiah did. He listened to God's call and agreed to convey God's plan. We know the outcome. Isaiah's people resisted the message; their kingdom fell; destruction ensued.

But that was not the end. From the demise of Israel and Judah and through the promises of God via the prophets, a new paradigm in salvation history emerged. The end Isaiah announced became a beginning. Beyond the hardening and darkness a bright new hope was already forming, a future even more majestic than anything that had previously been envisioned. That is what can happen when people answer God's call, when they agree to respond, as Isaiah did, "Send me."

For Discussion

1. Isaiah probably wasn't looking for the call that came when he went to the temple that day. Does that suggest that for us as well some of the most meaningful calls may come when we least expect them and by means that might surprise us?
2. Do humans cling to the concept of free will simply as a way to assert some sense of independence from all the overpowering forces of life, whether divine or earthly? What does "free will" mean to you anyway?
3. Isaiah was no super-being. God called and used him just as he was, right where he was, with the gifts he had at the meaningful moment. What could that mean for you? To what have you been called?

For Reflection

Try to hold these pieces together: (1) the part of your heart that's hard, that bears grudges, that resists forgiving, that would close off possibilities for others; (2) the part of yourself that needs to be free, to have a sense of choice and independence; (3) the part of you that longs for meaning, purpose, even recognition; (4) the unselfish, generous part of you that is willing to serve others. Wrap these pieces together. Lay them honestly before God. Consider how God might use them to guide or challenge you. Which piece needs addressing today?

For Prayer

Lord of new possibilities, help us to accept complexities beyond our understanding. Forgive our blindness and hardness of heart toward you and toward others. Open us to the prophetic calls life brings, and give us the trust and the courage to say, "Yes." Amen.

19

Existential Threat

"The heart of his people shook . . ."

ISAIAH 7:2 (RSV)

IN SOME WAYS OSAMA bin Laden was right. The ever-expanding influence of global culture, whether in the form of capitalism, pop music, or Western concepts of human rights, represents an existential threat to any fundamentalist religious worldview. Of course, militant fundamentalists with access to nuclear weapons constitute an existential threat to the entire global community. But, overall, in a world where women have ever-greater access to education and where the internet is available from cafes in rural Africa to laptops in the Arctic, it inevitably becomes increasingly difficult for isolation-based religious ideologies to endure.

Isaiah's community faced an existential threat as well, though not of the fundamentalist variety.

> In the days of Ahaz, the son of Jotham,
> son of Uzziah, king of Judah,
> Rezin the king of Syria
> and Pekah the son of Remaliah the king of Israel
> came up to Jerusalem to wage war against it . . .
> When the house of David was told,
> "Syria is in league with Ephraim,"
> his heart and the heart of his people
> shook as the trees of the forest shake before the wind.
> Isaiah 7:1–2 (RSV)

King Ahaz panicked, as did the general public of Judah. They trembled at the prospect of being over-run by this coalition of enemies, whose armies were already marching on Jerusalem. Understandably, one of the first things King Ahaz did was to check Jerusalem's defenses. For, in the military milieu of the ancient Middle East, city sieges were the key to conquest. King Ahaz had to ensure that the city walls were intact and especially that the water supply was secure enough to last through a prolonged onslaught. For, without water, the city would inevitably be forced to surrender.

> And the Lord said to Isaiah, "Go forth to meet Ahaz,
> you and Shearjashub, your son, at the end of the conduit
> of the upper pool on the highway to the Fuller's Field."
> Isaiah 7:3 (RSV)

It would be hard to represent God's engagement with humanity much more specifically than this, that is, God's naming the exact geographic location where Isaiah was to confront Ahaz. A God familiar with our water supplies and who knows the names of our landmarks trumps even GPS or a Google Earth map.

More importantly, however, God's instructions here typify a fundamental characteristic of biblical faith. The Hebrew people understood God to be deeply engaged in every aspect of human life, from sexuality (Adam and Eve) to construction project details (Solomon's temple, Noah's ark) to foreign affairs (Isaiah's prophecies). No wonder believers today operate with similar assumptions, almost as part of the DNA of their faith. The Hebrew model became a legacy passed on to Christians and Jews alike. Even Islamist terrorists witness to this view of God's familiarity with the details of daily life when they invoke divine judgment on particular targets.

The presupposition of God being actively engaged with human affairs is so embedded in monotheistic belief that it is easy to take for granted. Of course, there have been exceptions, including the deists among America's Founding Fathers who envisioned God's involvement in human affairs as distant and abstract, though even they signed on to the notion that God deliberately created humanity with equality in mind:

> "We hold these truths to be self-evident,
> that all men are created equal,
> that they are endowed by their Creator
> with certain inalienable Rights . . ."
> The Declaration of Independence, 1776

Isaiah's extensive prophecies regarding national foreign policy, then, should come as no surprise. For Isaiah's God was closely—even emotionally—engaged with public affairs and the existential threats to Isaiah's community. The reference to "the house of David" in this story reinforces the point.

The British "House of Windsor" (changed in 1917 from the house of "Saxe-Coburg-Gotha" in response to anti-German sentiments during WWI) is one of the last great royal families still in power in the world today, even if that power is more symbolic that actual. The Queen of England today may not order armies into battle or directly rule over far-flung empires as her forebears once did. But the royal line still holds a prominent place in the psyche of modern Britain (a recent BBC poll showed 78 percent of the British in favor of preserving the monarchy).

The idea of a "House of David" held even stronger sway in the national mythology of Judah, Isaiah's community. For centuries already, from the time when God had installed David on the throne of Israel with promises of a permanent Davidic line, the Hebrew people had believed that the survival of the nation would be ensured by the divinely blessed lineage of Davidic kings. That would hold true, they assumed, no matter how unfaithful or corrupt any particular king might be.

King Ahaz was a good test of that theory. His schizophrenic religiosity led him to chase after whatever god he thought might help him at the moment, even to the point of apparently incinerating his own sons to curry the divine favor of pagan gods (2 Chronicles 28:3).

Ultimately, in response to the failure of such a nationalized mythology, prophets such as Isaiah began expounding a new plan by which God would align the future well-being of the people of God not with a national entity but with a faithful community. Though the idea of a divinely blessed state has endured in the world for centuries—whether via the Holy Roman Empire, Conquistador Spain, or even a country such as the United States—all such states inevitably operate under the prophetic caveat that when the state engages in unrighteous behavior, its security is no longer assured.

Isaiah's own children embodied that message. When Isaiah met with Ahaz, God told him to take his son along. The poor boy probably had no clue when he walked to the well with his father that day that by virtue of his name he would come to symbolize a new historic reality for God's people and a frightening warning to King Ahaz. For, "Shearjashub" can be translated, "Only a remnant shall return." The clear message implicit in the boy's name was that the age of monarchy was over. Jerusalem would fall, as would the northern kingdom of Israel. The nation, as history proved, would soon be dissolved, its people dispersed and oppressed. Only a remnant would survive to eventually return to Jerusalem and start over. In the end, this theological declaration of "the remnant" became one of the most distinctive hallmarks of Isaiah's prophetic career. As symbolized by the boy Shearjashub, the God who engages so deeply in human history was about to initiate a game-changing strategy that would forever alter the history of faith. It would revolve around the foreign policy decision about to be made by King Ahaz.

For Discussion

1. How far can believers go in determining God's will in national and global affairs? How, among many competing viewpoints, can one discern which view is most likely to be correct?
2. It has been said that "The church is in great danger when it surrenders its freedom in the Gospel to a particular political stand" (Lutheran theologian Timothy Lull). How can one balance strong personal commitments to particular political positions with love for the neighbor who holds diametrically opposed positions?

For Reflection

Imagine yourself living in Jerusalem or a similar city in Isaiah's time. Marauding armies roam the land, periodically threatening your refuge. If your city falls, the young men will be killed, the women raped, the old abandoned, and nearly everyone left will be enslaved, possibly even led off to a distant land. Where is your hope? How do you maintain a coherent community and stable society? What values could hold your family and community together through both good times and bad?

For Prayer

All-seeing God, as you sent guidance by the prophets to your people long ago, give guidance and hope to the vulnerable and oppressed today. Strengthen the global community of faith that we may together endure the challenges of our times and together contribute to a future where justice, mercy, and peace prevail, where the vision you laid out through Isaiah is finally realized. Amen.

20

P.K.'s

"If you will not believe, surely you shall not be established."

ISAIAH 7:9B (RSV)

PASTOR'S KIDS, OFTEN REFERRED to as "P.K.s," are some of the few children in society categorized by their parents' profession. "Plumber's Kids" and "Pharmacist's Kids" just do not get the same recognition. Why?

Mostly, that has to do with the expectation that the children of clergy should somehow live up to the higher moral and behavioral standards that are associated with religious leaders. As spiritual leaders are put on a pedestal (often inappropriately), so, by extension, are their children—sometimes as much by their parents as by parishioners.

People who have grown up in small towns or close-knit communities understand this dynamic particularly well. Where everyone knows who belongs to whom, the acts of the children are associated with the family to which they belong. This can hold true not only for Pastor's Kids, but for children of the local doctor, school principal, business leader, and so on. Such children are warned not to engage in behaviors that would bring shame to the family reputation. The system does not always work. P.K.'s have something of a reputation for resisting, even rebelling against the unholy pressures of public expectations.

Isaiah's children faced similar pressure. Not only were they the offspring of a public prophet, but their father openly used them to buttress his religious proclamations. After all, what kind of kid would willingly choose to be named "Ma-her-shal-al-hash-baz," or, "The spoil speeds, the prey hastens" (Isaiah 8:3). One wonders what his mother called him and whether his friends came up with either a kinder or a more mocking nickname.

In biblical culture names had meaning. There may not have been as much stigma to the names Isaiah gave his children (at God's command) as there would be today. But that the children were destined for political and religious renown was clear:

> Behold, I and the children whom the Lord has given me are signs and portents in Israel from the LORD of hosts, who dwells on Mt. Zion.
> Isaiah 8:18 (RSV)

The children were markers, reference points to a critical, life-changing moment in the history of Israel's existence. As foreign armies laid siege to their world, their names would describe the course that both divine and human history was about to take.

King Ahaz, when met by Isaiah and his son She-ar-jash-ub ("a remnant shall return") had a decision to make. He could trust Isaiah's message from God that his enemies would fail in their efforts to conquer and depose him. Or he could take the agonizing political gamble of making a pact with his enemies' enemy, ensuring the survival of his kingdom but at the cost of turning it into a vassal state of the mighty Assyrian empire.

Interestingly enough, it is Isaiah—or, more to the point, God—who apparently brings news to King Ahaz that the kings of Syria and Ephraim are also plotting to replace Ahaz with a new king more amenable to their cause. In fact, they have already picked a successor.

> "Let us go up against Judah and terrify it, and let us conquer it for ourselves, and set up the son of Ta'-be-el as king in the midst of it . . ."
> Isaiah 7:6 (RSV)

Not unlike plotting politicians today, they thought they could affect the future of rival regimes. However, when addressing his followers, Isaiah says,

> "Do not call conspiracy all that this people call conspiracy,
> and do not fear what they fear, nor be in dread.
> But the LORD of hosts, him shall you regard as holy;
> let him be your fear, and let him be your dread."
> Isaiah 8:12–13 (RSV)

In the original Hebrew text the phrase about regarding God as holy can also be rendered as regarding God as the true "conspirator," or, in other words, the real architect behind the historical events taking place.

Ultimately, King Ahaz made the wrong decision. Instead of heeding Isaiah's counsel and trusting God, Ahaz aligned his fate with Assyria, saving his own skin and buying some time for his kingdom, but sealing its fate in the long run as a subjugated state.

Isaiah did not mince words about the consequences of such a decision. In a whole series of vivid images he described where this political folly would lead.

> In that day the Lord will whistle for the fly which is at the sources of the streams of Egypt, and for the bee which is in the land of Assyria. And they will come and settle in the steep ravines, and in the clefts of the rocks, and on all the thornbushes, and on all the pastures.
> Isaiah 7:18–19 (RSV)

To God, Isaiah infers, human armies are no more than swarms of insects that God can summon with a mere whistle, as one might summon a dog. So extensive is God's authority over all things earthly.

> In that day the Lord will shave with a razor which is hired beyond the River—with the king of Assyria—the head and the hair of the feet, and it will sweep away the beard also.
> Isaiah 7:20 (RSV)

In God's hands the mighty Assyrians will be just a sharpened blade that will shave Judah so bare it will be as if every hair on a person's body were removed.

> In that day every place where there used to be a thousand vines,
> worth a thousand shekels of silver, will become briars and thorns;
> Isaiah 7:23a, 25b (RSV)

The economic infrastructure will be ravaged; the good life, lost; the land itself, left in ruins. With an ironic justice, upper class and lower class distinctions will be erased as all will have to struggle equally to survive. When God was done with Judah and Israel, there would be next to nothing left: no state, no king, no cause for self-righteousness, no sense of superiority as a chosen people. Were it not for God's mercy, there would no longer be a chosen people at all.

> "Because this people have refused the waters of Shiloah
> that flow gently . . .
> therefore, behold, the Lord is bringing up against them
> the waters of the River,
> mighty and many, the king of Assyria and all his glory;

and it will rise over all its channels and go over all its banks;
and it will sweep on into Judah,
it will overflow and pass on, reaching even to the neck . . ."
Isaiah 8:6–8a (RSV)

The only seed of good news was the promise embodied in Isaiah's older son, She-ar-jash-ub, that, by God's grace, a remnant of God's people would survive and the hope of a new future would remain.

Ironically, in a purely political sense, Ahaz actually made a shrewd move. His deal with the Assyrians—including idolatrous accommodations to Assyrian religious beliefs—preserved the kingdom of Judah for another hundred years. Condemned by Isaiah and reviled by later biblical writers such as the author of the Book of Chronicles, Ahaz nevertheless survived his enemies and avoided the near-term destruction of his nation.

Isaiah, on the other hand, lost this prophetic battle with King Ahaz in the short run. Unable to persuade the king or the general public to heed his advice, Isaiah apparently withdrew from prophetic ministry for a time, either by choice or under pressure.

Bind up the testimony, seal the teaching among my disciples.
I will wait for the Lord, who is hiding his face from the house of Jacob, and I will hope in him.
Isaiah 8:16 (RSV)

Isaiah had been around long enough by this time to have gathered a personal following. If he could not change the course of public affairs, he could at least ensure that his prophecies would be recorded and collected for the day when they would be appreciated.

Previously Isaiah had ensured that his prophecies were properly witnessed and that they could be confirmed by events. "And I got reliable witnesses . . . to attest for me" (Isaiah 8:2, RSV). Isaiah understood the importance of testing prophetic proclamations against public events. In fact, Isaiah's prophecy about what would happen to Rezin of Syria and Pekah of the northern kingdom—the immediate threats to Ahaz which started this whole prophetic cycle—actually came true exactly as prophesied.

And I went to the prophetess, and she conceived and bore a son.
Then the Lord said to me, "Call his name Maher-shalal-hash'baz;
for before the child knows how to cry 'My father' or 'My mother,'
the wealth of Damascus and the spoil of Samaria will be carried away before the king of Assyria."
Isaiah 8:3–4 (RSV)

According to both biblical and extra-biblical sources, within just two years (about the amount of time it takes a child to begin to learn to make good and bad choices), that is exactly what happened to the kings who attacked Ahaz. They both met violent deaths and their people and goods were taken away captive.

King Ahaz would have seen the message of Isaiah's second prophetic child come true. But neither Ahaz nor Isaiah himself lived long enough to witness the full import of Shear-jashu'ub, the remnant-prophecy child. Nor could they have fathomed the extraordinary import of Isaiah's great prophecies about another child yet to come.

For Discussion

1. At one point Isaiah was beat, out of "sync" with the political momentum of his time. His government's policies conflicted with his most deeply held convictions about God's will for the nation. What are a believer's options in such circumstances?
2. Should clergy be put on a pedestal, not to mention their children? Why do people do it? What are the risks?

For Reflection

Put yourself in the place of King Ahaz. You and your people believe that you are threatened by a violent foe who will stop at nothing to harm or destroy you. Many religious leaders support your position. But a vocal minority call you to change your course of action, to base your national defense policy on a religious promise. How would you handle that?

For Prayer

Lord of history, guide us to make wise choices both as individuals and together as nations. Teach us to honor our children and the future they represent. Make us mindful of the inappropriate expectations we place on each other. Give us courage, constancy, and perspective for the living of our days. Amen.

21

Gloom and Deliverance

"But there will be no gloom for those who were in anguish."

ISAIAH 9:1A (NRSV)

THE CATALOGUE OF DARKNESS is staggering: Darfur, Rwanda, Cambodia, the Holocaust . . . the list goes on with numbing shame. How do we comprehend the descent of an overwhelming mass of destructive force on an entire population? The truth is we cannot. However, all of us have witnessed darkness in personal ways. We know how darkness may come in a tornado that takes a home, a predator that takes a child, an accident or disease that takes a loved one. We grieve the darkness of 9/11, Katrina, or the brutality of an horrific crime. But the sheer scale of darkness on a mass, murderous scale exceeds our capacity for comprehension. We can often only respond as did the people of Isaiah's time when Assyria obliterated the northern kingdom of Israel.

> They will pass through the land,
> greatly distressed and hungry;
> and . . . they will be enraged and will curse their king and their God,
> and turn their faces upward; and they will look to the earth,
> but, behold, distress and darkness, the gloom of anguish;
> and they will be thrust into thick darkness.
> Isaiah 8:21–22 (RSV)

It is a wonder people survive such times. Perhaps it is a wonder that the human race has survived at all, given our propensity for destruction. Then again, the global warming we have caused, together with the nuclear, biological and ever-improving space-based weaponry we are creating remind us that our future survival as a species on this planet is in no way guaranteed.

What can counter such gloom? Where does hope come from when we confront our instinct for annihilation?

> But there will be no gloom for those who were in anguish.
> In the former time he brought into contempt the land of Zebulun
> and the land of Naphtali,
> but in the latter time he will make glorious the way of the sea,
> the land beyond the Jordan, Galilee of the nations.
> The people who walked in darkness have seen a great light;
> those who lived in a land of deep darkness
> —on them light has shined.
> Isaiah 9:1–3 (NRSV)

As gloomy as Isaiah's prophecies of destruction could get, they were spectacularly transcended by his even more dramatic promises of hope and redemption. So powerful are the images of this particular passage that they have been woven into the fabric of faith for more than twenty-six centuries already.

Isaiah and his contemporaries could never have imagined the historical impact of these words. For them Isaiah's promise meant, first of all, a restored monarchy, that a king would arise who would liberate them from the Assyrian scourge. To Isaiah's first listeners who faced the imminent threat of an oppressor's yoke, blood in the streets, and a dismal future, Isaiah's words must have offered profound encouragement.

> You have multiplied the nation, you have increased its joy;
> they rejoice before you as with joy at the harvest,
> as people exult when dividing plunder.
> For the yoke of their burden, and the bar across their shoulders,
> the rod of their oppressors,
> you have broken as on the day of Midian.
> For all the boots of the tramping warriors
> and all the garments rolled in blood
> shall be burned as fuel for the fire.
> For a child has been born for us, a son given to us;
> authority rests upon his shoulders; and he is named
> Wonderful Counselor, Mighty God, Everlasting Father,
> Prince of Peace.
> His authority shall grow continually, and there shall be endless peace
> for the throne of David and his kingdom.
> He will establish and uphold it

> with justice and with righteousness from this time onward
> and forevermore.
> The zeal of the Lord of hosts will do this.
> Isaiah 9:3–8 (NRSV)

When kings were crowned in the ancient world, these were the kind of words used in public pronouncements. Egyptian pharaohs typically had five royal names associated with their ascension to the throne. In Isaiah's prophecy there are four plus a hint of a fifth in old manuscripts. Some scholars believe that Isaiah's prophecy was prepared for Hezekiah, the king who came after Ahaz and who embodied the ideals associated with a true and faithful leader. But as it turned out, Isaiah's prophecy came to mean far more.

In 1741 an Englishman named Charles Jennens—somewhat of an outcast from the elite society of his day due to his political preferences—penned a libretto for a composer he admired. Jennen's idea was to set a series of biblical passages to music to be sung in an oratorio form. The composer he befriended, a temperamental German with a hefty paunch, a thick accent, and a certain renown for being able to curse in five languages, was a recently bankrupted opera composer about to give up on trying to make a living in England.

Impressed by Jennen's idea, however, the composer George Friedrich Handel withdrew into the seclusion of his lodgings and in just twenty-four days completed a 260-page composition that some have called "the greatest piece of Christian music ever written." Handel's servant, it is said, left food outside the door while Handel was composing, often returning to find it barely touched until the day that Handel emerged with tears in his eyes, supposedly just after completing the "Hallelujah" chorus, proclaiming "I did think I did see all Heaven before me, and the great God himself!"

First performed in Dublin, Ireland in 1742, Handel's "Messiah" drew such crowds that women were asked not to wear hoop skirts to the concert hall and men not to wear their swords so that there would be more room for audiences to pack in. English audiences, on the other hand, took longer than the Irish to appreciate Handel's masterpiece. Even Jennens himself was not only disappointed but vowed to "put no more sacred works into his hands, thus to be abused." In contrast, Ludwig von Beethoven personally hand-copied every word and note of Handel's later much-revised manuscript so as to absorb it in more depth. Beethoven called Handel "the greatest composer that ever lived." Today, thanks to

Handel's "Messiah," the words of Isaiah's great prophecy, "For unto us a child is born . . ." are literally sung out across the globe in both secular and religious performances.

It is critical to note that in Isaiah's original vision the new era, when "of the increase of his government and of peace there will be no end," will be one upheld "with justice and with righteousness" as opposed to one upheld by violence and coercion: "the boot of the tramping warrior in battle tumult and every garment rolled in blood will be burned as fuel for the fire." At its core, the new reality will be fundamentally different from the world we now know in which humans dominate and exploit each other by force, one in which darkness stains human existence.

Not surprisingly, Isaiah's subsequent readers have related Isaiah's prophecies to their own historical situations. The connection between Isaiah's specific mention of "Galilee of the nations," for example, in relation to a great light "in the latter time," and the appearance of Jesus of Nazareth, raised in Galilee, is probably history's greatest example. The very geographic area which first fell to the Assyrian conquerors became the precise region in which deliverance first emerged in the eyes of the early Christians. But to them that dawn was spiritual, not political, totally transcending the traditional concepts of kingship and the previous meaning of David's throne while at the same time being associated with the Davidic line through Jesus's father, Joseph. Similarly, Galilee represented an intersection of the "nations," or, the non-Jewish world not only in Isaiah's day, but also in Jesus's day, perhaps foreshadowing the multi-ethnic character which came to typify Jesus's later followers as Christianity spread into the Greek and Roman world. For Jesus, too, as his followers would witness, the gloom of crucifixion gave way to the overwhelming power of resurrection and the recognition of a light which no darkness could ever overcome.

In the midst of dark times Isaiah promised God's people that they would one day be able to say, "The people who walked in darkness have seen a great light." For as long as darkness continues to infect human existence, Isaiah's great tribute to the light will continue to inspire human hope.

For Discussion

1. Isaiah's people knew both the physical and the spiritual geography of their heritage. When Isaiah mentioned Naphtali or Galilee, for example, they understood the implications both past and present. Do we know the stories we need to know? Are we familiar enough with the "geography" of our spiritual heritage that we can discern the great sweep of God's active presence in our own time?
2. Handel's Messiah is even more remarkable in light of its conception: the simple idea of an undistinguished but well-off Anglican with a chip on his shoulder presented "out of the blue" to an inauspicious Lutheran musician who was trying to eke out a living in a country that was not even his own. Such greatness from such happenstance! What does that suggest about the possibilities present in every human encounter?

For Reflection

In a world where science delves into the subatomic levels of matter and where both technology and the media fragment life into ever smaller "bits" of experience and information, what happens to a sense of wholeness? We can choose either to highlight the uniqueness of each moment or to see its inter-connectedness with all that has preceded and shaped it. Reflect on the greater pattern of your life. What elements of your existence—your name, your ethnicity, your genetic predispositions—connect you not only to an extended family but to an entire community and a social history? How does what you are doing just today—whether drinking a cup of coffee or reading these words, for example—link you to the human community as a whole? From Isaiah to iPods, does history strike you as a series of unrelated pieces or as an integrated, purposeful whole?

For Prayer

Gloom-dispelling God, liberate us from all the ideologies and obsessions which oppress us. Drive out the forces of darkness from our hearts and from our world. Excite our imaginations with the vision of a world at peace, where light, creativity and joy permeate our days. Amen.

22

Virgins

"Behold, a young woman shall conceive . . ."

ISAIAH 7:14 (RSV)

BY SOME ACCOUNTS, THE Buddha was born out of the side of his mother. Popular Buddhist lore even held that the Buddha was immaculately conceived and that his mother, Mahamaya, died seven days after his birth as part of a cosmic plan to ensure the perpetual purity of her womb.

In one form or another virgin birth has been associated with great religious figures for centuries. Nearly two thousand years before Jesus was born, the cult of Egypt's pharaohs included virgin birth stories, as did the god stories of ancient India. Greek, Roman, and Minoan cultures associated extraordinary births with both mythical and historical figures ranging from Dionysus (the god of wine) emerging from the thigh of Zeus to the philosopher Plato himself being the product of a virgin's womb. So widespread was the idea of extraordinary, virgin-related birth that some scholars suggest that the birth narratives of the Buddha may have derived—along with the use of statues to depict the Buddha—in part from Buddhist encounters with Greek culture via Alexander the Great's invasion of India in the third century BCE.

In Hebrew faith the idea of God's "birthing" Israel and of God causing special leaders to be born even from barren wombs (e.g., Sarah: Isaac; Hannah: Samuel), runs throughout the Hebrew Scriptures. But it is with Isaiah that the issue of a virgin birth first emerges. What the prophet Isaiah actually thought about virgin birth, however, is a matter of considerable debate.

> "Therefore, the Lord himself will give you a sign.
> Look, the young woman is with child and shall bear a son,
> and shall call his name Immanuel."
> Isaiah 7:14 (NRSV)

The Gospel of Matthew quotes this passage from Isaiah in relation to the birth of Jesus. In English we read "a virgin shall conceive and bear a son, and his name shall be called Immanuel" (Matt 1:23a, RSV). Of course, this English is itself a translation of the original Greek text of Matthew's Gospel, which was based on the Hebrew word originally used in the Isaiah text. There is the rub. Does the original Hebrew word, *almah*, actually mean virgin as we understand the term today? Scholars disagree. Some define *almah* as a young woman of marriageable age who may or may not be a virgin. Some say it just means sexually mature. Others argue that it could refer to a woman who is married (and thereby not a virgin) but who has not yet had children. Predominantly, however, the preference (among Christians, at least) has been to understand Isaiah's prophecy in light of the Christian belief in the virgin birth of Jesus because *parthenos*—the Greek word used to translate *almah*—uniquely means virgin.

What is often overlooked in this understandable association of Isaiah's prophecy with Jesus's birth—especially with its reference to "Immanuel"—is the original context:

> "For before the child knows how to refuse the evil
> and choose the good,
> the land before whose two kings you are in dread will be deserted."
> Isaiah 7:16 (RSV)

Isaiah's prophecies were all given in the context of historical reality. Some of his prophecies clearly transcended those realities, offering warning, instruction, and hope to later believers. But in the case of King Ahaz and Isaiah's Immanuel prophecy, there was originally a very targeted message. Judah's King Ahaz was faced with a life and death political decision. The very existence of his nation and people was threatened. Even God's long-standing promise of permanent support for the house of David seemed at risk.

Isaiah offered encouragement. In fact, the text says that God, too, spoke directly to Ahaz to offer a sign of assurance as part of an ongoing dialogue designed to persuade Ahaz to listen to and to trust in God's protection. Ahaz, however—the self-serving, manipulative, hypocritical politician that he was—tried to weasel out of God's offer in order to pursue his own agenda. An angry, frustrated Isaiah responded with a blast meant to chasten Ahaz publicly.

> "Hear now, you house of David!
> Is it not enough for you to try the patience of men?
> Will you try the patience of my God also?
> Therefore the Lord himself will
> give you [plural in Hebrew] a sign."
> Isaiah 7:13–14a (NIV)

Signs were a significant feature of Hebrew religious tradition. Since creation itself God had been sending signs from the miraculous to the mundane, from the reassuring rainbow after the great flood to the frightening plagues in Egypt. If a virgin were pregnant, that would constitute a remarkable sign indeed. Whether she was already pregnant or would soon conceive (the text has been interpreted both ways), this was a pregnancy that was meant to be noticed. In this prophecy before King Ahaz, Isaiah specifically refers to "the" *almah*, implying that the king and his court knew the woman. Some say it was a woman already selected to become one of Ahaz's wives or concubines. Some have even speculated that she was a wife of the prophet Isaiah, who, after all, was already known for giving his children symbolic names. Whoever she was, the naming of her son Immanuel—God with us—conveyed multiple messages.

To Ahaz and the fearful people of Jerusalem the Immanuel message furnished a remarkably specific time frame in which their distress would be relieved—roughly two years, or the time it takes a child to develop sufficiently to "reject the bad and choose the good," at least on an elementary level such as in behavioral choices or food preferences. But the Immanuel promise carried a mixed message as well. It did not guarantee that no harm would come to Ahaz and his people. The God who provided the sign of Immanuel was the same God who was about to

> "bring on you and on your people and on your ancestral house
> such days as have not come
> since the day that Ephraim departed from Judah
> [a time of division and civil war]—the king of Assyria."
> Isaiah 7:17 (NRSV)

The name Immanuel (God-with-us) could have been given either as an encouragement for trying times or as a recognition after-the-fact that the community had survived, thanks to God's faithful presence. In a similar manner the references to "curds and honey" in the Immanuel prophecy ("He shall eat curds and honey when he knows how to refuse the evil and choose the good"—Isaiah 7:15, RSV) also carried ambiguity. To the early Israelites who were desert nomads, curds and honey were a symbol of the Promised Land, of settled, peaceful life, even luxury. On the other hand, to a people whose agrarian economy was about to be destroyed by an invading army, curds and honey could signify all that would be left for a subsistence, survival diet. This component of the sign of the Immanuel prophecy could even refer to the restoration of social justice and a national chastening as the survivors of a fallen kingdom were "liberated" from the corruptions of power and class and placed on a more egalitarian, survive-together-or-die footing.

So, what happened to the baby, not to mention the mother? If little Immanuel lasted long enough to eat curds and honey, he must have survived the political turmoil of his infancy and perhaps even served as a symbol of God's promise and presence. Does the fact that we hear nothing more about him suggest that he was not the product of a publicly recognized virginal conception after all? Usually, a person marked for such renown from conception receives special attention. Then again, perhaps the point of Isaiah's Immanuel sign has less to do with virgin birth than with another message.

The heart of Isaiah's prophecy could simply be—as we see so consistently throughout Scripture—that: (a) God takes the initiative to steer us towards trust in God's plans, and, (b) God repeatedly gives reassurances of being present, whether in the trials of a nation or in the life of an individual. Ours is the challenge to heed the warnings and the guidance we receive and to trust in the divine presence offered.

For Discussion

1. Who would you choose to be in the Immanuel encounter: (a) Ahaz, the leader responsible for existential decisions; (b) Isaiah, the irritating prophet full of righteous indignation; (c) the *almah*, caught up in events over which you had no control, or (d) Immanuel, the God-carrier, without your knowledge or consent, seen mainly as a symbol by others?

2. What meaning does virgin birth have for you? What role, if any, does it play in your faith?

For Reflection

How would you define God's presence in your life? What are the "signs" you could point to as markers, either large or small, that have provided direction or comfort—whether or not those were recognizably from God? Make a list. Create an actual inventory for as far back as you can remember of the people, experiences, events, lessons, etc., that might have been signs. Look for patterns. Do some signs occur more than others? What kinds of signs register most with you?

Share your list. See what signs others would include, both for themselves and for you, especially if they know you well. Look together for any signs in the social or political realm that might indicate God's activity. Use Isaiah's standards, not just your own preferences, as a measure: God's promises, God's call to faithfulness, and God's deep passion for justice and peace.

For Prayer

Dear "With-us God," open our minds and our hearts to your presence. In that presence may we find deep peace. From that peace may we take confidence for all that lies ahead. This we pray in Immanuel's name. Amen.

23

God's *Dabar*

"The Lord has sent a word against Jacob, and it will light upon Israel . . ."

ISAIAH 9:8 (RSV)

"AND NOW FOR A word from our sponsor" is one of the most familiar phrases in television history. "Pastor, could you say a word?" is one of the most common requests clergy receive. Clergy words are solicited for prefacing everything from meals to graduation ceremonies, from military campaigns to football games. It is as though the words that come out of the mouths of a religious leader somehow have more value than the words of an ordinary believer, or as if clergy, by virtue of their religious education, have access to a spiritual vocabulary or to a connection with the holy that is unavailable to ordinary mortals. Or, maybe clergy are simply society's "designated prayers," given their religious role and presumed expertise.

In any case, if the praying clergy offers a few too many words of blessing or commentary, listeners fidget, eager to move on to what actually holds greater meaning at the moment. Perhaps prayer requests of clergy in life's more mundane moments are thought to serve as a hedge against the possibility that there is a necessary power to be recognized or appeased, or that a verbal tribute to the holy will bestow blessing and good order, much as a magical incantation might. Of course, it must be recognized that for many people, such prayers do embody genuine devotion.

"The Lord has sent a word against Jacob, and it will light upon Israel" (Isaiah 9:8, RSV). Isaiah's use of "a word" was entirely different. He understood the true power involved when the speaker of a word was God. For God's word was no benign blessing or passive pleasantry. When God spoke, things changed, not always for the better. The word God sent to "light upon Israel" was a frightening, devastating, horrific word.

Therefore the anger of the Lord was kindled against his people,
and he stretched out his hand against them and struck them . . .
and their corpses were like refuse in the streets . . .
the Lord raised adversaries against them . . .
The people did not turn to him who struck them . . .
So the Lord cut off from Israel head
and tail . . . elders and dignitaries . . .
and prophets who teach lies . . .
for those who lead this people lead them astray . . .
That is why the Lord did not have pity on their young people,
or compassion on their orphans and widows;
for everyone was godless and an evildoer,
and every mouth spoke folly . . .
For wickedness burned like a fire . . .
Through the wrath of the Lord of hosts
the land was burned, and the people became like fuel for the fire . . .
For all this his anger has not turned away;
his hand is stretched out still."
Isaiah 5:25, 9:11–22 (NRSV)

Five times the refrain is repeated in Isaiah's recounting of the causes for the destruction God has decreed: "For all this his anger is not turned away and his hand is stretched out still" (Isaiah 5:25; 9:12, 17, 21; 10:4, RSV). How bad must things be for God to have no compassion even for orphans (v. 17)? Could that happen to us? Could we as humans so violate the bounds of human decency and responsibility that God would speak a word of obliteration against the entire human race? Is that what cataclysmic Armageddon prophecies reflect? Will the accumulations of world wars, genocides, gulags, enslavements, and exploitations one day lead us all to be "fuel for the fire" or to be "corpses lying as refuse in the street"?

Or is that over-reaching? Is Isaiah's imagery limited to a prophetic reading of only his own times, offering a theological framework for interpreting the civil wars, corruption, and ultimate destruction coming upon the Northern kingdom of Israel with the invading armies of the Assyrians? We might even ask if it was fair either to God or to the people of Israel for the prophet to pin their doom entirely upon their own behavior. We know that to do so can be an effective preaching device for motivating people to change their ways. We also know that this causal perspective of sin and punishment was the lens through which the Old Testament prophets viewed history's unfolding.

But how does that relate to us today? Is God's hand "stretched out still" to hold us accountable? Many would probably say "yes," but would they apply that principle to Darfur, to terrorism, to starving children and HIV/AIDS, to profiteering and corruption in financial markets, or to global environmental destruction? Could those activities trigger God's sending a word against us, or are they the word already sent? Or, are they not related to God's word at all? How do we know what God's word is today anyway?

To be sure, most Christians are adept at invoking "the word of God." Mainline Protestants and Catholics listen to lectionary readings of the "word of God" every Sunday and reply "Thanks be to God" even when the words read—if seriously considered—are often quite discomforting. "Word Alone" (derived from *Sola Scriptura*) is the phrase that Lutheran Christians have clung to for five centuries to assert the primacy of Scripture (God's biblical Word) as the core document for their beliefs. Churches everywhere these days name themselves "Word of . . . (this or that) Church" in an effort to identify themselves as rooted in biblical teaching or truth. Pastors of all stripes announce in ponderous and dramatic tones that they are conveying the "Word" of God. In sizeable segments of the global Christian community the Word of God has been expropriated as an exclusive possession tied to particular theological interpretations which often end up dividing believer from believer and becoming a weapon of condemnation and intolerance towards those who view God's Word differently.

Could Isaiah have related to such views of God's Word? For prophets such as Isaiah, the "Word" of God (*dabar* in Hebrew) was a powerful, dynamic force, too complex to be contained in doctrinal formulas. When the prophets said, "the word of the Lord came" to them, it was testimony to an all-consuming power that overwhelmed and redirected their lives. In the biblical view the *dabar* of God is more like "the Force" of *Star Wars* than it is simply a bibliographic reference for a theological treatise or sermon. God's Word is alive, transformative. It can be healing or destructive, but always it is effective.

> "Is not my word like fire, says the Lord,
> and like a hammer which breaks
> the rock in pieces?"
> Jeremiah 23:29 (RSV)

> The word of God is living and active,
> sharper than any two-edged sword,
> piercing to the division of soul and spirit, of joint and marrow,
> and discerning the thoughts and intentions of the heart.
> Hebrews 4:12 (RSV)

To the Psalmist the Word of God was "a lamp to my feet and a light to my path" (Psalm 119:105, RSV). "The grass withers, the flower fades; but the word of our God will stand forever" (Isaiah 40:8, RSV).

So full of meaning is "the word of God" in Scripture that the noun *dabar* in Hebrew is used more than 1400 times in the Old Testament and was translated in eighty-five different ways in just the King James version of the Bible, referring to everything from the Ten Commandments (Ten "Words") to the history ("word-acts") recorded in the Book of Chronicles. Finally, the Gospel of John in the New Testament opens with the majestic text portraying the culmination of God's Word as the Incarnation, capturing both the Word's creative power and its relational expression:

> In the beginning was the Word, and the Word was with God,
> and the Word was God. He was in the beginning with God;
> all things were made through him,
> and without him was not anything made
> that was made. In him was life and the life was the light of men.
> The light shines in the darkness,
> and the darkness has not overcome it . . .
> And the Word became flesh and dwelt among us,
> full of grace and truth . . .
> John 1:1–5, 14 (RSV)

Ultimately, the Word of God exceeds our ability to describe it. As a living power, it cannot be contained. "And now for a word from our sponsor" is a phrase that should actually send chills down the spine of anyone who hears it—at least for those who believe that God is in fact the ultimate "sponsor" of human life, history, and destiny. When it comes to the Word of God, it would seem wise to give heed.

For Discussion

1. What does the "Word of God" mean to you and where did you get your definition?

2. Can God's living word find expression in multiple faiths, such as Christianity, Judaism, Islam, Buddhism, etc.?

For Reflection

A Taiwanese theologian has said that the use of the Greek term *logos* by early Christians to translate the Hebrew term *dabar* in New Testament writings was a disastrous idea. For, the Greek term incorporates a rationality and ultimately an empirical expectation that diminished the wild, organic power inherent to the Hebrew experience of God's Word.

Indeed, it is true that intellectually we are heirs of Enlightenment rationalism, struggling with the tensions between faith and reason. We want proof, predictability and control. Emotionally, however, the choices we make when it comes to such things as politics, war, romance, religion, and even finances continually contradict what reason would imply. Spiritually, we drift between fundamentalism and unbelief, searching for a faith that can integrate the disparate pieces of our lives, providing an assurance of meaning and purpose, or at least a calming center.

What a fertile situation for the Word of God! Imagine such a living force penetrating your world. Let the dynamic presence of the Word which has survived the rise and fall of empires and which has been there in the darkest and the brightest moments of human history be present for you. Visualize God's Word seeping into your soul or billowing around you, reshaping, redefining, revealing in new ways all aspects of life. Through time spent in Scripture, prayer, and spiritual conversations, explore how the *dabar* of God can become a word which grounds and directs your life anew. What word has God spoken for you?

For Prayer

Origin of all words, give us fear that we might recognize and yield to the awesome power of your living Word. Instruct us in that word so that we might live meaningful, faithful, gracious lives. Send words of warning as necessary and healing where needed to the places of conflict, pain, and injustice in our human community. Plant your Word within each one of us that we might become living words to each other for the redemption of our world. Amen.

24

The Remnant of Destruction

"Destruction is decreed, overflowing with righteousness."

ISAIAH 10:22B (RSV)

"BEWARE OF EDITORS," A disgruntled writer friend once advised. "They'll mess with your text." Biblical scholars understand exactly what that means. The many editors who assembled and arranged the collection of writings which we call the Bible often "messed with the text" in the process of preparing God's written word for their communities of faith over the centuries.

The opening verses of the tenth chapter of Isaiah are a good example. Attentive readers can readily discern that pieces of text which seem to belong together are distributed over several different chapters. Verses 24–30 of chapter 5, verses 8–21 of chapter 9, and verses 1–5 of chapter 10 could all fit nicely together as a single prophecy directed at Israel, warning of the Assyrian invasion, united by the repeated refrain, "For all this his anger is not turned away, and his hand is stretched out still."

So why did the editor(s) stick part of the prophecy at the beginning of what we call chapter 10? Perhaps their intent was to create a transition from one topic to another in a particularly pointed way. Isaiah's words served as a kind of two-edged sword. One edge of the blade continued to cut at the corruption of Israel; the other sliced into the arrogance of the conquering Assyrians, proclaiming their inevitable doom as well.

> When the Lord has finished all his work on Mt. Zion
> and on Jerusalem
> he will punish the arrogant boasting of the king of Assyria
> and his haughty pride.
> Isaiah 10:12 (RSV)

But before elaborating on God's judgment of Assyria, Isaiah's editors wanted to ensure that his prophecy against his own people was complete. Ironically, that prophecy included writers (and, implicitly, editors!) whose work contributed to oppression.

> Woe to those who decree iniquitous decrees,
> and the writers who keep writing oppression,
> to turn aside the needy from justice
> and to rob the poor of my people of their right,
> that widows may be their spoil,
> and that they may make the fatherless their prey!
> Isaiah 10:1–2 (RSV)

What does it mean to "decree iniquitous decrees" and who are the "writers who keep writing oppression"? In Isaiah's day as in ours, legal codes (or lack thereof) which favored the interests of the privileged at the expense of the vulnerable would be an obvious example. According to prophetic logic, human laws actually matter in God's eyes. The governing documents and legal frameworks adopted by nations and organizations have a moral impact. If financial regulations, judicial processes, and the fair treatment of individuals—especially the vulnerable—are compromised, then not only is human community damaged but divine values are violated as well. Ultimately, Isaiah prophesies, exploitation will be met with judgment:

> What will you do on the day of punishment,
> in the storm which will come from afar?
> To whom will you flee for help, and where will you leave your wealth?
> Nothing remains but to couch among the prisoners
> or fall among the slain.
> Isaiah 10:3–4a (RSV)

Do not the lessons from Isaiah's day still apply? For believers today the world is just as integrated. The regulations of global financial markets, international agreements, the U.S. Patriot Act, the American Constitution, civil rights legislation, environmental regulations—all these embody either God's justice or God's inevitable judgment. That certainly held true for the Assyrians:

> Ah, Assyria, the rod of my anger, the staff of my fury!
> Against a godless nation I send him,
> and against the people of my wrath I command him . . .
> But . . . his mind does not so think;
> Isaiah 10:5–7 (RSV)

The Assyrians never understood. They did not comprehend their place in divine history. Not unlike empires even into modern times, they viewed their historical ascendancy as the product of their own efforts, their political, religious, and military superiority. As Isaiah depicted their perspective:

> "By the strength of my hand I have done it, and by my wisdom,
> for I have understanding;
> I have removed the boundaries of peoples,
> and have plundered their treasures;
> like a bull I have brought down those who sat on thrones."
> Isaiah 10:13 (RSV)

In their own minds the Assyrians even saw themselves as the victors in a war of religions:

> "As my hand has reached to the kingdoms of the idols
> whose graven images were greater than those of Jerusalem
> and Samaria,
> shall I not do to Jerusalem and her idols
> as I have done to Samaria and her images?"
> Isaiah 10:10–11 (RSV)

God had a response to such delusion:

> "Shall the ax vaunt itself over the one who wields it,
> or the saw magnify itself against the one who handles it?
> As if a rod should raise the one who lifts it up,
> or as if a staff should lift the one who is not wood!"
> Isaiah 10:15 (NRSV)

The Assyrians mistakenly believed that they were the masters of their own fate when in fact they were but instruments in the hand of a greater power.

Over against the hubris of the Assyrians, Isaiah's prophecy began to turn away from the gloom that would befall God's faithless people to the hope that lay beyond.

> In that day the remnant of Israel and the survivors
> of the house of Jacob
> will no more lean upon him that smote them,
> but will lean upon the Lord,
> the Holy One of Israel, in truth.
> A remnant will return, the remnant of Jacob,
> to the mighty God.
> Isaiah 10:20–21 (RSV)

This was both good news and bad news. On the one hand, God was promising forgiveness and deliverance from the horrors of Assyrian conquest:

> "For in a very little while my indignation will come to an end,
> and my anger will be directed to their destruction."
> Isaiah 10:25 (RSV)

But the cost would be high:

> For though your people Israel be as the sand of the sea,
> only a remnant of them will return.
> Isaiah 10:22a (RSV)

One of the greatest promises in Scripture was God's extraordinary declaration to Abraham that one day his descendents would number as the stars of the heaven and the sand on the seashore (Genesis 22:17). Now, after centuries of expansion, after God's chosen family had grown from a single nomadic clan to a multitude exiting Egypt to a population sufficient to establish two nations, God was about to reduce them to a remnant again, to a powerless, vulnerable, chastened shadow of their previous glory.

> "Destruction is decreed, overflowing with righteousness."
> Isaiah 10:22b (RSV)

A remnant would indeed persist well beyond the Assyrian conquest to eventually return from Babylonian captivity. The record of their illustrious religious and national history would survive. The words of prophets such as Isaiah, the stories of the kings and the people, the creation accounts, the inspiring poetry of the Psalms and Proverbs, the accounts of Egyptian captivity and the migration to the Promised Land—all these would last, even though the nation was ultimately destroyed and the people dispersed. Today, nearly thirty centuries later, the records of that remnant people form the basis of faith for nearly a third of the earth's population. Assyria, the "ax that would vaunt itself," turned out to be a footnote to the history of the remnant people, not the other way around.

As Isaiah declared, destruction was decreed, but righteousness prevailed as a testimony to a Creator God who demands justice but who continually holds out the hope of restoration, even when rejected. The Assyrians are long gone. Isaiah is dead. But the images, stories, and promises he left us still stir the soul and guide the faithful. Some even say that the remnant of which Isaiah spoke turned out to be us: the keepers of biblical faith today, which makes for a whole new understanding of the meaning of "remnant." In the end, Isaiah's prophecy described humanity's future in a way far more profound than Isaiah himself could ever have imagined.

For Discussion

1. Do you buy the argument that the policies of governments, corporations, schools, churches, and other organizations that might "decree iniquitous decrees" can be held accountable to prophetic standards?
2. How do you react to the prophetic notion of "righteous destruction"? In God's dealing with the wayward people of Judah is God a surgeon excising a cancer to enable the patient to survive? Is God the Cosmic Editor messing with the text to write a better ending? Or are you so uncomfortable with this kind of story that you have to consign it to a primitive religious past and refuse to accept God on those terms today?

For Reflection

Has God been messing with your text? Look back at the story of your life. Recall the early editors: your parents, your siblings, teachers, your community. Review the chapter headings: childhood, high school, travel, your job history, key relationships. Where has there been destruction? Did righteousness eventually emerge? What is God writing or editing in your life now? How do you want the story to end?

For Prayer

God, our Author and Redeemer, write with your loving hand across the pages of our lives. Read your grace into our stories. Edit out our iniquities with a righteousness that cleanses, renews, and redirects our lives, so that what remains in our story at the end of the day will be a witness to faithfulness, justice, and compassion. Amen.

25

Trees, Beasts, and Peace

"The earth shall be full of the knowledge of the Lord"

ISAIAH 11:9 (RSV)

No one today has an Yggdrasil tree growing in their backyard. No one ever did. The Yggdrasil, or "World Tree" from Nordic mythology, was supposedly a giant ash tree which sheltered vast worlds within itself. Like the Sacred Tree of Celtic tradition, the Yggdrasil was the axis of reality, the connection point between past and present, gods and humans, myth and reality. From time immemorial, it seems, sacred trees have played a vital role in shaping the religious consciousness of human beings. From the Tree of Life in the garden of Eden to the Bodhi tree of the Buddha, trees have symbolized life, mystery, and the interwoven nature of reality. Even in the oft-unnoticed, tongue-twisting "Proper Preface for Lent" in the Christian communion liturgy, a tree signifies the connection between life and death:

> "It is indeed right and salutary
> that we should at all times and in all places
> offer thanks and praise to you, O Lord, holy Father,
> through Christ our Lord;
> who on the tree of the cross gave salvation to all,
> that where death began,
> there life might be restored, and that he,
> who by a tree once overcame, might by
> a tree be overcome."

Perhaps not surprisingly, destroying the symbolic tree of an adversary has long been a potent expression of military, cultural, and religious domination. In the early 700s CE a Christian bishop named Boniface gained fame by felling the sacred "Oak of Thor" near Geismar in modern day Germany through a "trial by ordeal," which persuaded the locals to accept the Christian god. As far back as the days of Isaiah, the image of godly power being demonstrated by the destruction of an enemy's forest was familiar.

> Behold, the Lord,
> the Lord of hosts will lop the boughs with terrifying power;
> the great in height will be hewn down,
> and the lofty will be brought low.
> He will cut down the thickets of the forest with an axe,
> and Lebanon with its majestic trees will fall . . .
> The remnant of the trees of his forest will be so few
> that a child can write them down.
> Isaiah 10:33–34, 19 (RSV)

Isaiah's prophecy went beyond the mere physical destruction of the timbers that fed the war machines and built the temples and palaces of Assyria—or of Judah, for that matter. Isaiah was describing the decimation not only of religious and political opposition but even the hewing down of the Davidic family tree, the royal lineage which served as the foundation for Judah's existence as a nation. However, Isaiah added a twist. After making the point that Judah's security could no longer reside in human institutions, Isaiah introduced a new promise.

> There shall come forth a shoot from the stump of Jesse,
> and a branch shall grow out of his roots.
> And the Spirit of the Lord shall rest upon him,
> the spirit of wisdom and understanding,
> the spirit of counsel and might,
> the spirit of knowledge and the fear of the Lord.
> And his delight shall be in the fear of the Lord.
> Isaiah 11:1–3 (RSV)

Amazingly, in this prophetic pronouncement rooted in political events from a bygone century Christians have long discerned a precursor to Christmas. For, Jesse, the man referred to in this passage was both the father of the great king David and associated with the humble town of Bethlehem. As the words of a classic fifteenth century German hymn put it,

"Lo, how a Rose e'er blooming from tender stem hath sprung;
of Jesse's lineage coming as men of old have sung . . .
Isaiah 'twas foretold it, the Rose I have in mind.
With Mary we beheld it, the Virgin Mother Kind,
to show God's love aright, she bore to men a Savior,
when half spent was the night."
Translated by Theodore Baker in 1894

In a paradigm consistent throughout Scripture Isaiah describes God as bringing life out of death, victory out of defeat, as creating something out of nothing, taking what is weak and insignificant and turning it into something stupendous. To Isaiah's original listeners, still thinking in the same old patterns, this simply meant the coming of a new king, one with all the best qualities associated with a divinely appointed monarch. But to later listeners Isaiah's prophecy pointed to a future beyond anything originally imagined.

To begin with, the Spirit of the Lord would directly define this exceptional figure, this branch of Jesse. *Ruach*, the Hebrew word used here for Spirit—the very breath of God—is the same word used for the Spirit of God moving over the face of the waters at Creation (Genesis 1:2). This creative spirit would bring what Solomon had prayed for centuries earlier when he was crowned as king:

"And now, O Lord my God, you have made your servant king . . .
Give your servant therefore an understanding mind to govern your people, able to discern between good and evil . . ."
1 Kings 3:7, 9 (NRSV)

Kings in Old Testament times were often considered to have special abilities bestowed on them by the gods. What is particularly interesting about Isaiah's prophecy is the emphasis it gives to wisdom, to a king being able to resolve disputes with insight and good judgment instead of violent conflict. Even the phrase "counsel and might" used in this passage carries the implication of diplomatic skill over raw power. Indeed, the "spirit of wisdom and understanding, the spirit of counsel and might, the spirit of knowledge and the fear of the Lord" lead directly to the stunning utopian vision that soon follows the announcement of the coming shoot of Jesse.

The wolf shall live with the lamb,
and the leopard shall lie down with the kid,
the calf and the lion and the fatling together,

and a little child shall lead them.
The cow and the bear shall graze;
their young shall lie down together;
and the lion shall eat straw like the ox.
The nursing child shall play over the hole of the asp,
and the weaned child shall put its hand on the adder's den.
They will not hurt or destroy on all my holy mountain,
for the earth will be full of the knowledge of the Lord
as the waters cover the sea.
Isaiah 11:6–9 (NRSV)

Edward Hicks (1780–1849) may not be a household name. But his many renditions of the "Peaceable Kingdom" were a hit in nineteenth-century America. A self-taught painter of signs and carriages, this Quaker preacher painted perhaps a hundred versions of Isaiah's idyllic vision. Living in an age when America was a young country, expanding across an Eden-like continent, it must have seemed like Isaiah's vision might in some way be actually achievable.

Eden restored, a paradise where violence, conflict, and death are no more—is this not the longing of every human who has suffered life's brutalities, whether in the ancient Near East or in the cataclysmic devastations of the last one hundred years? "Knowledge and fear of the Lord," for Isaiah, was the key to unlocking this appealing new reality.

Ironically, that same "knowledge and fear of the Lord" was exactly what was absent in the portions of prophecy which were probably attached by later authors to Isaiah's great vision. For the transition from universal harmony to renewed bloodletting was almost immediate.

> In that day . . . they [Judah and Ephraim]
> shall swoop down upon . . .
> the Philistines in the west,
> and together they shall plunder the people of the east.
> Isaiah 11:14 (RSV)

Unless one believes that Isaiah's prophecy of peace applied only to a very limited geographic area (God's holy mountain), then it is obvious that the vengeful thinking of a violent past soon trumped Isaiah's image of a peaceful future. With an irony as striking as Isaiah's vision of the wolf and lamb lying together in peace, the wolf is once more unleashed to devour its prey.

Two different mindsets, it seems, collide in these passages. The mind of reconciliation is countered by the mind of aggression. To this day, both mentalities continue to exist. On the one hand we see the instincts which drive human beings to seek things like international peace, the eradication of poverty, and the preservation of species and natural environments. On the other hand we suffer the instincts of vengeance, ideological conflict, and a disregard for life, played out from the mountains of Pakistan to the jungles of the Congo to the corporate board rooms and political capitals of modern states. The truth is, even on an individual level most of us wrestle with the self-centered instincts that lead to conflict over against the inclinations to self-sacrifice that contribute to Isaiah-like harmony.

In such a scenario, where does hope lie? For Isaiah the answer was clear. To know the God who can sprout new life out of a nearly dead stump, who can birth Eden out of chaos, and who can make a lion eat straw—to know such a God as this is to already be on the way to discovering the peaceable kingdom.

For Discussion

1. The ideal figure, as described by Isaiah, "shall not judge by what his eyes see, or decide by what his ears hear" (11:3b). Isn't this how we all would like to be judged? Do you ever wish that people would see you not in terms of outer appearances or measure you not by what others say, but rather with more awareness of your inner identity? How could that happen?
2. "For the earth shall be full of the knowledge of the Lord as the waters cover the sea" (11:9b). Do you think that what Isaiah is depicting here is a time when one religion will have achieved dominance over all others in a sort of cosmic religious contest? Is knowledge of the Lord confined to only one human faith system? Or does what Isaiah is referring to transcend anything we have so far imagined?

For Reflection

"With righteousness he shall judge the poor, and decide with equity for the weak of the earth . . ." (11:4a). There it is again—Isaiah's (God's) concern for the poor, the vulnerable, the lambs being hounded by wolves. Which are you—lamb or wolf? Both? What would it mean for the lion in you to learn to eat straw? Would it mean consuming less energy or fewer material goods? Would it be biting your tongue more in interpersonal disputes? Would "deciding with equity for the weak of the earth" mean advocating for the voiceless in your community, helping to build a Habitat home, or becoming an International Monetary Fund banker to assist Third World countries with loan guarantees?

"The leopard and the kid," the "calf and the lion," the "cow and the bear shall feed, their young shall lie down together . . ."—these are images of power and vulnerability, side by side. What does that suggest for your career objectives, your political leanings, your friendships and family dynamics, your inner need to recognize and balance assertiveness and vulnerability, your strengths and your weaknesses? How can Isaiah's vision of harmony become a guiding image for your daily life?

For Prayer

O Lord of lambs, wolves, and promises, send us a spirit of wisdom. Help us to see through external appearances to internal truths in order to be more just and compassionate in how we treat one another. Open our minds to a vision of peace and a level of harmony beyond our ordinary imaginings. Excite us with expectation as we move towards that day when the earth, full of the knowledge of the Lord, will be a place where "they shall not hurt or destroy" anyone, anywhere, anymore. Amen.

26

Miriam Dancing

"With joy you will draw water from the wells of salvation."

ISAIAH 12:3 (RSV)

MOSES HAD A BIG sister. We know that from the account of his sister standing in the reeds at the river bank watching over her baby brother as he floated in a basket on the Nile (Exodus 2:1–10). What many people do not realize is that she reappears later in the chronicles of Moses at significant moments.

In fact, Moses sister, Miriam by name, along with her other brother, Aaron, at one point actually turns on Moses, apparently resentful of his prominence and offended by one of his cross-cultural marriages (Numbers 12:1). Miriam and Aaron both claim authority for themselves, saying, "Has the Lord indeed spoken only through Moses? Has he not spoken through us also?" (Numbers 12:2, RSV).

In a depiction of sibling rivalry as dramatic as anything the ancient Greeks or Shakespeare could have imagined, Moses, Miriam, and Aaron are summoned to stand before the Almighty to face judgment. In no uncertain terms God informs Miriam and Aaron that Moses remains the preeminent one. Then, an angered God turns Miriam into a hideous leper. Her brother Aaron immediately intercedes, pleading with Moses to ask for God's mercy, which Moses does. But God declares that Miriam must still suffer by being cast out of the community of God's people, which meant that her very survival was at risk (Numbers 12:4–16).

We do not know if friends in the Israelite camp smuggled food or water or medicine out to Miriam to help her survive. But her enduring importance to the community is demonstrated by the storyteller's note that "the people did not set out on the march till Miriam was brought in again" (Numbers 12:15).

If we were looking at this story through feminist eyes, would we see Miriam as unfairly stigmatized by a patriarchal tradition? Would we not wonder why she and not Aaron was punished so severely? Would we not celebrate her courage not only in challenging Moses for his marital behavior but also for protecting him at the river all those years ago where she had to face another powerful woman in order to save her brother's life? As a woman to whom God had spoken, could we not imagine Miriam today as a popular televangelist with a large, devoted following? Then again, why are we talking about Miriam anyway in the context of Isaiah's prophecies?

> And there will be a highway from Assyria
> for the remnant which is left of his people,
> as there was for Israel when they came up from the land of Egypt.
> Isaiah 11:16 (RSV)

Egypt, slavery, Exodus—these were fundamental shaping images for the Hebrew people, paradigms for understanding their identity and place in the world. The God who delivered Moses from the river, the God who liberated an entire people from oppression—this was the God who could also deliver Isaiah's people from the Assyrians.

> "Behold, God is my salvation;
> I will trust, and will not be afraid;
> for the Lord God is my strength and my song,
> and he has become my salvation."
> Isaiah 12:2 (RSV)

The word, "salvation," in Hebrew (*yesa* in its various forms) literally refers to being "brought out" to a spacious place, or, simply, "to go out," especially as in God bringing out the Israelites from Egypt. At the Red Sea, after witnessing the watery destruction of an entire army of one of the world's superpowers of that day, the Israelites literally broke into song to celebrate their being "brought out" not only physically but also symbolically to a place spacious enough for them to become a new people. Miriam, Moses's sister, was the one who led the rejoicing.

> Then Miriam, the prophetess, the sister of Aaron,
> took a timbrel in her hand;
> and all the women went out after her with timbrels and dancing.

And Miriam sang to them;
"Sing to the Lord, for he has triumphed gloriously;
The horse and his rider he has thrown into the sea."
Exodus 15:20–21 (RSV)

The song of thanksgiving recorded in Isaiah reiterates Miriam's famous words, "Sing to the Lord, for he has done gloriously" (Isaiah 12:5). In fact, the phrases of this song repeat the words of the Psalmist as well:

The Lord is my strength and my song;
he has become my salvation.
Psalm 118:14 (RSV), echoed in Isa 12:2b

The words in these passages are identical because they were embedded in the consciousness of the Hebrew people. As Isaiah's song demonstrates, they were preserved in poetic and liturgical formats designed to keep them alive.

"You will say in that day . . .
And you will say in that day . . .
Sing praises . . .
Shout and sing for joy, O inhabitants of Zion . . ."
Isaiah 12:1a, 4a, 6a (RSV)

As instructions for teaching or for community worship, these directions helped people to remember the defining moments of their past. Whether or not Isaiah personally composed this thanksgiving song at this point in the book that goes by his name, it remains consistent with his primary message. For all his prophecies of judgment and doom, Isaiah aimed to steer his people back to trust, to a recognition of the saving power of God.

You will say in that day:
I will give thanks to you, O Lord,
for though you were angry with me,
your anger turned away,
and you comforted me.
Isaiah 12:1 (NRSV)

The One who had pronounced judgment on Israel and Judah, who had allowed their destruction, was also the One who ensured that a remnant would survive, who promised not only a restoration of Spirit-led leadership but a glorious new day when all destruction and suffering would end. Incredibly, the very One by whose anger they were chastened would become the One to bring them comfort.

Many scholars see chapter 12 in the book of Isaiah as a demarcation point, a form of closure for the first portion of Isaiah's work. Isaiah's life and work as a prophet have been introduced; the historical situation has been laid out; Isaiah's prophecies of condemnation and hope to the wayward descendants of the Exodus have been delivered. Ironically, after all the angst and turmoil in the previous chapters, this chapter turns the focus to thanksgiving, to celebrating the deliverance of the promise-keeping God.

The chapter ends with an exhortation to share the good news, to sing, shout, and let it be known throughout the earth that "great in your midst is the Holy One of Israel." The true expression of gratitude, it seems, is witness. One can almost see Miriam, timbrel in hand, dancing still.

For Discussion

1. Do you have any "defining events" or key reference points comparable to the Hebrew's Exodus experience in your faith community or personal experience? Or is faith in the modern context so individualistic and so focused on the "now" that we resist the authority of previous experience? Either way, what memories are essential to preserving your faith?
2. What makes you thankful when it comes to matters of faith? Does your gratitude extend to witness? If not, is it deep enough?

For Reflection

"With joy you will draw water from the wells of salvation" (Isaiah 12:3). How deep is your well? How much joy does it give you? What kind of salvation does it hold? For some people, salvation today is holding onto their home in a devastated mortgage market. For others on the planet it is simply finding enough food to survive another day. What would it feel like to go deeper, to discover a wellspring of deliverance and hope that would trigger internal joy even when external reality is grim?

Look into your well. Do you see light dancing on the water, or mostly shadows, auguring a sense of something there, but indistinct? Read 4:7–15 in the New Testament Gospel of John about Jesus's encounter with the Samaritan woman at a well. Then contemplate "living water" and what it would mean to thirst no more, to be free of life's nagging desires, demands, and anxieties. Savor in your imagination the sensation of a sip of cool water on a hot day or of a fine wine in a beautiful setting, a moment of satisfaction, when life seems in balance, complete, with nothing more required (at least for that moment). Now picture a well of salvation filled to the brim with such moments.

For Prayer

Wellspring of salvation, we give thanks for all that is known, for all witnessing to joy, for the promise of wells overflowing with deliverance. Bring us out to spacious places where we may be recreated and refreshed by your living water. Empower us to sing. Teach us to praise, that we, too, may give witness to hope wherever it is needed, joined to Miriam and Isaiah and the song they offered: "Sing praises to the Lord, for he has done gloriously; let this be known in all the earth." Amen.

27

Globalization

"Hark, an uproar of kingdoms, of nations gathering together!"

ISAIAH 13:4B (RSV)

CONTRARY TO COMMON PERCEPTIONS, the United States of America is one of the oldest countries in the world. While the size and scope of the national entity known as the United States has changed considerably over the last two and a quarter centuries, the form of government has remained relatively constant. In fact, as a political entity, the United States has become one of the most enduring enterprises in human history.

There are older civil societies, to be sure. Egypt—even more than China—is one of the very oldest of these, having a widely recognized, fairly coherent cultural, political, and geographic identity dating back over 5000 years. But its governance structure has often varied. Likewise, the United Kingdom is frequently thought of as having one of the most widely recognized cultural and geographic identities and one of the world's most enduring systems of governance in history. Yet the composition and relationships of its component peoples (e.g., Scottish, Welsh, Irish, British, etc.) have shifted significantly over the centuries (even into the nineteenth century), as has the locus of power in the ebb and flow between monarchical rule and parliamentary democracy. Iceland, strikingly, has what is considered to be the world's oldest legislative assembly, the *Althing*, established in 930 CE. Iceland itself, however, has been alternately independent and subject to continental rule.

But many older entities such as these, along with most current countries in the world, have arguably experienced more systemic political upheaval than has the United States in the last two hundred years. Most of the African, Asian, and South American nation-states that we know today did not even exist in anything like their current form until well after the United States was at least fifty years old. Countries like Saudi Arabia, Nigeria, and Pakistan did not come into being until after the United States had been around for 150 years. (Of course, it must be noted that native peoples constituted "nations" in many places—including North and South America—even during the last two centuries, though generally in terms quite different from the common understanding of political states today.)

Switzerland was a recognized confederation within the Holy Roman Empire for over six hundred years before it adopted a constitution and federal form of government in 1848. By then the United States had had eleven presidents and a federal government with a constitution for over sixty years. When Thailand's multilingual Western-oriented King Mongkut wrote to Abraham Lincoln offering to send Thai battle elephants to fight for the Union Army in the Civil War, the American Presidency was only six years younger than the king's entire monarchic line.

Russia was still ruled by a Czar when Teddy Roosevelt became the twenty-sixth president of the United States and when the Wright brothers flew the first airplane at Kitty Hawk in 1903. By the time most European nations emerged from the monarchical rule of Europe's royal households (some such as Spain as recently as the 1930s with a constitution only first passed in 1975), the United States had been a democracy for nearly a hundred years.

When Franklin Roosevelt became the thirty-second president, the Korean peninsula was still under the colonial rule of Japan, as most Southeast Asian nations and parts of China already were or soon would be. Already Vietnam had been a French colony for nearly fifty years and India at the time still had a British Empress. Some portions of modern-day Australia had only recently ceased receiving convicts as British penal colonies when South Dakota joined the century-old Union in 1889. France, Italy, and most Middle Eastern and Balkan states have turned over governments multiple times since the United States began its long run as a stable, constitutional democracy.

Whether by its fortunate geography as part of a separate continent, or by a confluence of rich natural resources, creative political thinking, timely leadership, or other such factors, the fact remains that the United States has persisted—despite a devastating Civil War—as one continuous nation. Never successfully invaded, never occupied (a few brief incursions during the War of 1812 notwithstanding, even though the British held and burned Washington, DC for a day in 1814), uninterrupted by coup or conquest, the United States stands nearly alone in the annals of world history as a uniquely consistent national entity.

The same cannot be said for Assyria, Babylonia, or the other world powers that arose in the days of Isaiah and other biblical prophets. As great as Assyria became, it was constantly torn with political strife. Its borders expanded and contracted with countless skirmishes and wars. Its leaders changed by assassination as well as by paternal succession. Yet Assyria dominated the world of its day for nearly two hundred and eighty years, shaping the destinies of people across the Middle East, including the people of Israel.

Babylonia, in turn, did the same, but for a much briefer period. The era of Babylonian dominance lasted less than one hundred years, making it all the more ironic that Babylon became a metaphor for oppressive regimes, especially since the Assyrians committed far more atrocities. Yet in the New Testament book of Revelation it is Babylon that serves as a euphemism for the might and corruption of Rome (e.g., Revelation 18, referring to Isaiah 13 and 22). During the Protestant Reformation it was Babylonia that theologians such as Martin Luther invoked as a symbol of religious oppression (e.g., in "The Babylonian Captivity of the Church" in 1520 CE). Babylon retains, more than its ancient peers, a place in literary and political discourse to this day.

It was over against the tumultuous period of Assyrian and Babylonian ascendancy that the writing of great biblical prophets such as Isaiah and Jeremiah took shape. Chapters 13–23 in the book of Isaiah paint a picture of this ever-changing historical tapestry. Not all of what we find in these chapters comes from Isaiah himself, though his core teachings percolate throughout this portion of the book which bears his name. Some prophecies reflect themes and archetypes that were already familiar in Isaiah's day and upon which he built, as did others after him. Isaiah 14:3–21, for instance—one of the most vitriolic yet satirical passages in all of Scripture—describes with relish the fate of an arrogant ruler brought low, a sentiment understandable in the violent and oppressive times endured by generations of Isaiah's people.

"Sheol beneath is stirred up to meet you when you come,
it rouses the shades to greet you,
all who were leaders of the earth . . .
all of them will speak and say to you:
'You too have become as weak as we! You have become like us!'
Your pomp is brought down to Sheol, the sound of your harps;
maggots are the bed beneath you, and worms are your covering . . .
How you are cut down to the ground,
you who laid the nations low!
You said in your heart, 'I will ascend to heaven,
above the stars of God . . .
I will make myself like the Most High.'
But you are brought down to Sheol, to the depths of the Pit.
Those who see you will stare at you, and ponder over you:
'Is this the man who made the earth tremble, who shook kingdoms,
who made the world like a desert and overthrew its cities,
who did not let his prisoners go home?'
All the kings of the nations lie in glory, each in his own tomb;
but you are cast out, away from your sepulchre,
like a loathed untimely birth, clothed with the slain,
those pierced by the sword,
who go down to the stones of the Pit,
like a dead body trodden under foot."
Isaiah 14:9–20 (RSV)

Biblical prophecies were often layered with history, created in one context, then dusted off and reapplied to another (e.g., portions of chapters 13, 21, and 22 could have been applied to both Assyria and Babylon). In a similar way believers today continue to reinterpret Scripture in order to apply it to the ever-changing circumstances in which we live.

Isaianic prophecies of judgment and destruction expressed the frustrations, sufferings, and longings for relief, even vengeance, that were natural given the traumatic experiences of the times the prophets addressed.

Wail, for the day of the Lord is near;
it will come like destruction from the Almighty, it will come! . . .
See, the day of the LORD comes, cruel, with wrath and fierce anger,
to make the earth a desolation and to destroy its sinners from it . . .
I will punish the world for its evil, and the wicked for their iniquity;
I will put an end to the pride of the arrogant,
and lay low the insolence of tyrants.
I will make mortals more rare than fine gold . . .
Isaiah 13:6–12a (NRSV)

At the same time, prophecies of restoration witnessed to faith in a God who was active in human history and putting things right:

> The Lord will have compassion on Jacob
> and will again choose Israel and will set them in their own land . . .
> When the LORD has given you rest from your pain and turmoil
> and the hard service with which you were made to serve . . .
> Isaiah 14:1, 3 (RSV)

Prophecies of deliverance not only renewed hope, providing encouragement in difficult times. They also testified to faith in God's promises to God's people: "On that day people will regard their Maker, and their eyes will look to the Holy One of Israel" (Isaiah 17:7, NRSV).

In Isaiah's original writings we see a persistent "Purpose Theology," reassuring proclamations that God has a plan and will accomplish it.

> The Lord of hosts has sworn:
> "As I have planned, so shall it be,
> and as I have purposed,
> so shall it stand,
> that I will break the Assyrian in my land,
> and upon my mountains trample him underfoot;
> and his yoke shall depart from them
> and his burden from their shoulders.'
> This is the purpose that is purposed concerning the whole earth;
> and this is the hand that is stretched out over all the nations.
> For the LORD of hosts has purposed, and who will annul it?
> His hand is stretched out, and who will turn it back?"
> Isaiah 14:24–27 (RSV)

The nations listed in these chapters are numerous, ranging from the great empires such as Babylonia, Assyria, and Egypt to such powers as the Medes, the Ethiopians, the Phoenicians, Syrians, and Philistines, along with an array of less powerful players such as the peoples of Moab, Edom, Arabia, and the like. All the references to and prophecies about such surrounding nations witness to a growing awareness among Isaiah's people of the ethnic and political multiplicity in which they lived.

> Hark, a tumult on the mountains as of a great multitude!
> Hark, an uproar of kingdoms, of nations gathering together!
> The LORD of hosts is mustering a host for battle.
> They come from a distant land . . .
> Isaiah 13:4–5a (RSV)

This oracle reveals more than a picture of apocalyptic consequences ("they come . . . to destroy the whole earth"—Isaiah 13:5b). It connects the people of other lands to God's intentions: "I myself have commanded my consecrated ones, have summoned my mighty men to execute my anger, my proudly exulting ones" (Isaiah 13:3, RSV), referring not to Israel but to her enemies! Implicitly these verses also portray the real-life encounters of Isaiah's people with previously unknown races and tribes on the field of battle, due to the fact that the Assyrians conscripted peoples from the various tribes and ethnic groups which they conquered across the ancient world to serve in the advancing ranks of their invading armies.

We today can understand better than any people who have ever lived the full impact of inter-ethnic, inter-cultural, and international encounter. Throughout world history, through wars and trade, civilizations have often met, from Solomon's trade with the Queen of Sheba on the Horn of Africa, to the movement of silk from China to Egypt to adorn Cleopatra in the first century BCE, to the trade ships of England and Spain carrying spices, gold, and slaves in the seventeenth century.

For centuries wars have frequently been inter-ethnic: Persian versus Chaldean, Chinese versus Mongol, Aryan versus proto-Indian, European versus Asian, and more. But it is only with the dawn of modern media and transportation, combined with truly global military and economic interests, that the peoples of the world have been connected *en masse*. Events in India or Gaza are beamed into homes from Minnesota to Moscow to Buenos Aires in real time. Global markets share a common calendar and trading system. Average citizens from any given country can end up studying, traveling, or receiving medical attention half a world away.

"Globalization" is the word we use to refer to all the implications of the modern world, whether protested in the streets, planned in global financial gatherings, or celebrated in the world's Olympic Games. A glimmer of globalization is what triggered the prophecies we read in Isaiah, a response to the conflicts and experiences of a people facing a world in transition. They needed a theology to address and interpret their experience, just as we do today.

The prophets provided it. They declared judgment on exploitation and unfaithfulness; they affirmed God's continuing presence and purpose. By their pronouncements on international events they placed those events squarely within the realm of the Creator God's activity. No less than Isaiah's audience, we are the heirs of that perspective. Our theologies today are more global than ever, responding to the international, inter-ethnic, and inter-cultural realities we face in our time. With Isaiah and the prophetic tradition as a guide, we should be richly prepared for whatever lies ahead.

For Discussion

1. Is globalization God's will? Is what we are seeing in the world today the unfolding of God's design for human history? Or does such a view simply overlay religious ideas on an inevitable progression?
2. All the great religions seem to have universal components. In some Islamic thinking all babies are born Muslim and then most fall away, captured by errant or incomplete religious traditions. The ideal future in such a vision is the ultimate recognition of Islam by all peoples as the consummation of God's revelation, reflected in the global *ummah* (community of believers) of the submitted (*muslim*).

Christians express a similar perspective, claiming Jesus as God's ultimate self-revelation and the church as God's servant people on earth. Buddhism, in turn, offers a way of enlightenment open to all people, as already subscribed to in one form or another across most of Asia and in many pockets of Western society as well.

For all these religions, the confluence of technology-based information-sharing and unprecedented opportunities for interpersonal encounter is rife with potential. Where will this lead?

For Reflection

Look at a world map. Picture the peoples that inhabit the spaces outlined by lines that were often drawn for political reasons. When you focus on the peoples, what is your gut reaction to the multitude of cultures and colors that you can envision? Fear? Excitement? Stress? Conflicts of culture and creed continue to define so much of our lives, just as in Isaiah's day. How does your faith impact your reaction?

For Prayer

Lord of time, the currents of history swirl around us in patterns beyond our comprehension. In sorrow we watch some people drowning in the floods of destruction, while others comfortably drift in calmer waters. Give us the consolation of a meaningful direction to the flow. Steady our boats for the journey, and help us to cast life lines to one another rather than pushing others under. Finally, help us to trust that your hand is on the rudder, steering all time and all people towards safe and peaceful shores. Amen.

28

The Naked Prophet

> "In the year that the commander in chief, who was sent by Sargon the king of Assyria, came to Ashdod and fought against it and took it—at that time the Lord had spoken to Isaiah son of Amoz, saying, 'Go, and loose the sackcloth from your loins and take your sandals off your feet,' and he had done so, walking naked and barefoot."
> Isaiah 20:1–2 (NRSV)

IF THE PROPHET ISAIAH were to return today and engage in some of the same behaviors he pursued in his own day, he would be arrested for indecent exposure, committed to psychiatric care, and probably branded as a sex offender. Appearances would dictate consequences. Form would trump substance, as if often does in contemporary culture. Tragically, Isaiah's prophetic message would be missed. Fortunately for us, the people of his own day got the point.

Around 713 BCE "the inhabitants of this coastland" (Isaiah 20:6), the Philistine people who lived around the Mediterranean coastal city of Ashdod, were plotting a revolt against Assyria. Judah's king Hezekiah, the successor to Ahaz, was sympathetic, but apparently heeded Isaiah's warning to steer clear of direct involvement. Egypt, Ashdod's neighbor to the south, had recently been taken over by Ethiopians, the first time in a thousand years that Egypt had been ruled by a foreign dynasty. Flush with success but still smarting from a defeat in a serious skirmish with an Assyrian army near Syria, the new leaders of Egypt assured the peoples of Ashdod that Egypt would "have their backs" when the Assyrians came calling.

Poor Ashdod. They got creamed by the Assyrians. The Ethiopian-Egyptians not only abandoned Ashdod but turned over to the Assyrians their rebel leader who had fled to Egypt for sanctuary.

Isaiah saw it coming. More to the point, God did, which raises the interesting question of why God sent a prophet with a message for the Philistines and through them for the Egyptians and Ethiopians. Perhaps the answer is that the message was really meant for King Hezekiah and the people of Judah, warning them not to form political alliances that could backfire, but rather, to place their trust in the only One who could truly deliver them.

The people of Jerusalem, however, did not learn the lesson of Ashdod. Despite three years of Isaiah's street theater (scholars still debate as to whether he was totally naked or just walking around in skimpy underwear), Hezekiah decided just ten years later to form an alliance with Egypt and other neighbors to break free from Assyrian rule. It didn't work. Hezekiah's kingdom was devastated by Assyrian armies, Jerusalem was surrounded, and less than forty years later, the Ethiopian rules of Egypt were completely crushed and replaced via Assyrian conquest. What happened to Egypt was pretty much what Isaiah prophesied.

> Then the Lord said, "Just as my servant Isaiah
> has walked naked and barefoot for
> three years as a sign and a portent against Egypt and Ethiopia,
> so shall the king of Assyria lead away the Egyptians captives
> and the Ethiopians
> as exiles, both the young and old, naked and barefoot,
> with buttocks uncovered,
> to the shame of Ethiopia.
> And they shall be dismayed and confounded
> because of Ethiopia their hope
> and of Egypt their boast.
> In that day the inhabitants of this coastland will say,
> 'See, this is what has happened to those in whom we hoped
> and to whom we fled
> for help and deliverance from the king of Assyria!'"
> Isaiah 20:3–6 (NRSV)

There is a double "bang for the buck" in this account, because Isaiah's prophetic actions as described here were tapped twice, once around 711 BCE and again around 701 BCE when facing further Assyrian aggression, to make a point to the people of Judah. Plus, this whole episode invites us deeper into the story of what was happening to Judah's neighbors around that time. Chapters eighteen and nineteen of the book of Isaiah discuss extensively the relationship between Judah, Egypt, and Egypt's Ethiopian rulers. Isaiah, for example, describes the exchange of messengers and ambassadors between Egypt and Jerusalem as the two governments coordinated the rebellions.

> Ah, land of buzzing insects, beyond the rivers of Ethiopia,
> sending ambassadors by sea,
> in papyrus boats on the waters!
> Go, swift messengers,
> to a nation tall and bronzed,
> To a people dreaded near and far,
> a nation strong and conquering . . .
> Then will gifts be brought to the LORD of hosts from a people tall and bronzed . . .
> to Mt. Zion where dwells the name of the LORD of hosts.
> Isaiah 18:1–2, 7 (NAB)

Parts of chapter 19 provide details about Egypt's internal affairs. The descriptions there of civil war in Egypt:

> I will stir up Egyptians against Egyptians,
> and they will fight, one against the
> other, neighbor against neighbor,
> city against city, kingdom against kingdom . . .
> Isaiah 19:2 (NRSV)

A government and a society in chaos:

> The Lord has poured into them a spirit of confusion;
> and they have made Egypt stagger in all its doings
> as a drunkard staggers around in vomit . . .
> Isaiah 19:14 (NRSV)

Combined with natural disasters along the Nile and consequent economic collapse:

> The waters of the Nile will be dried up . . .
> its canals will become foul . . .
> And all that is sown by the Nile will dry up . . .
> Those who fish will mourn . . .
> the workers in flax will be in despair . . .
> and all who work for wages will be grieved . . .
> Isaiah 19:5–10 (NRSV)

And a repressive ruler:

> I will deliver the Egyptians into the hand of a hard master;
> and a fierce king will rule over them, says the Sovereign the Lord of hosts.
> Isaiah 19:4 (NRSV)

All these images reflect a striking familiarity with Egyptian life and culture by Isaiah and his counterparts, both in Isaiah's own lifetime and in the decades that followed. Tragically, from the prophet's perspective, the Egyptians, despite their great heritage of knowledge and technological innovation, had never been able to discern that their fate was ultimately in the hands of Isaiah's God.

> The princes of Zoan are utterly foolish;
> the wise counselors of Pharaoh give stupid counsel.
> How can you say to Pharaoh, "I am one of the sages, a descendant of ancient kings?"
> Where now are your sages?
> Let them tell you and make known
> what the Lord of hosts has planned against Egypt.
> Isaiah 19:11–12, NRSV)

What stands out as unique, however, after all the oracles of judgment and doom are pronounced, is a picture of Egypt and—shockingly—even Assyria as someday co-existing in harmony with Israel. In fact, it is prophesied that the Egyptians will eventually join the community of God's faithful followers and be blessed and chastened in the same way as the Hebrew people.

> The Lord will make himself known to the Egyptians;
> and the Egyptians will know the Lord on that day,
> and will worship with sacrifice and burnt offering,
> and they will make vows to the Lord and perform them.
> The Lord will strike Egypt, striking and healing;
> they will return to the Lord,
> and he will listen to their supplications and heal them.
> Isaiah 19:21–22 (NRSV)

Most amazing of all is the prophecy that Egypt and Assyria will partake in the blessing promised to Abraham that by him all the families of the earth would be blessed (Genesis 12:3).

> On that day Israel will be the third with Egypt and Assyria,
> a blessing in the midst of the earth,
> whom the Lord of hosts has blessed, saying,
> "Blessed be Egypt my people,
> and Assyria the work of my hands, and Israel my heritage."
> Isaiah 19:24–25 (NRSV)

Given all the prophecies of judgment and destruction, all the images of brutality and suffering contained in this prophetic book, it is astounding to see such a glimmer of reconciliation and peace. But there it is. Does it reflect a fantasy born of despair or a confidence based on faith? Considering the tension and conflicts of today's world, either response could apply to our times as well.

For Discussion

1. If God were to tell you to run around naked in public, what would you do? More to the point, how far are you willing to go in your social setting to witness to God's presence and concern for the people around you?
2. The prophetic task was intensely political in Isaiah's day. Faithfulness to God was either revealed or betrayed in political decisions. Our context differs, does it not? Our governments are not as entwined with divine selection as was the faith-based monarchy of Isaiah's day. Is that good or bad? Does Isaiah's application of religious principles to political choices offer a model for believers today? What are the pros and cons as you see them?

For Reflection

Intriguingly, the book of Isaiah mentions all kinds of animals:

> "The wolf shall dwell with the lamb . . .
> the calf and the lion . . . the cow
> and the bear . . ." (Isaiah 11:6ff.)

> "And I will make it a possession of the hedgehog . . ." (Isaiah 14:23a)

"But wild beasts will lie down there,
and its houses will be full of howling
creatures [or, 'a haunt of hoot owls,' as some translators put it] . . .
there ostriches will dwell, and there satyrs
['he-goats' in other translations]
will dance. Hyenas will cry in its towers,
and jackals in the pleasant palaces . . ."
(Isaiah 13:21–22, RSV)

"Like fluttering birds, like scattered nestlings,
so are the daughters of Moab . . ."
(Isaiah 16:2, RSV)

"They shall all of them be left to the birds of prey of the mountains
and to the beasts of the earth . . ." (Isaiah 18:6a)

Was Isaiah the Francis of Assisi of the Old Testament, a man keenly attuned to the animal kingdom? Or, was such sensitivity to nature just typical of a people who lived close to the land and its non-human inhabitants? Either way, what does that suggest for our attention to the role of earth's creatures in God's activity in the world today? Do animals, fish, birds, and the like figure in your visions of the human future? If you have a pet, or if you can see birds or animals out your window, focus your attention on them for a while and ponder.

For Prayer

God of the Nile, God of our cities and markets, God of oceans, continents, governments and nations, God of our technologies, our knowledge and arts, expand our minds to envision the scope of your engagement with the human race. Free our thinking to embrace the rich possibilities before us as peoples and nations, imagining a day when by you all the families of the earth will be blessed, along with the earth itself and all its creatures. Amen.

29

Politics as Usual

"Let us eat and drink, for tomorrow we die."

ISAIAH 22:13B (RSV)

MARTIN LUTHER WAS ONCE asked what he would do if he knew he were going to die the next day. "Plant a tree," was his famous reply. How many of us would say the same? Would we not more likely answer, "Spend my remaining time with loved ones," or simply, "Pray"? To be perfectly honest, some of us would opt for "party like there's no tomorrow." That is what the people of Jerusalem did.

> In that day the Lord God of hosts
> called to weeping and mourning,
> to baldness and putting on sackcloth;
> but instead there was joy and festivity,
> killing oxen and slaughtering sheep,
> eating meat and drinking wine.
> Isaiah 22:12–13 (NRSV)

Jerusalem was in mortal peril. In 701 BCE the armies of Sennacherib, the new king of Assyria, were on the rampage in Judah. King Hezekiah had just been given an ultimatum: surrender or die.

Isaiah counseled Hezekiah to pay more attention to God than to Sennacherib. Already Isaiah had cautioned the king against joining the Egyptians and other neighbors in the revolt that had now brought the Assyrians to their city gates. But Isaiah's counsel had been overruled by political decision makers. King Hezekiah, a popular and heroic figure, had done his best to restore Jerusalem's prestige, cleansing the temple, destroying idols, holding the biggest Passover celebration in living memory:

So there was great joy in Jerusalem,
for since the time of Solomon the son of David king of Israel,
there had been nothing like this in Jerusalem.
2 Chronicles 30:26 (RSV)

Hezekiah had rebuilt Judah's army and prepared Jerusalem for a siege, even commissioning what is now called Hezekiah's tunnel—one of the most striking engineering feats of its time and still a wonder to tourists today—to channel water into the city.

And when Hezekiah saw that Sennacherib
had come and intended to fight against
Jerusalem, he planned with his officers
and his mighty men to stop the water of
the springs that were outside the city . . .
and they stopped all the springs and the
brook that flowed through the land, saying,
"Why should the kings of Assyria
come and find much water?"
2 Chronicles 32:2, 4 (RSV)

Hezekiah rebuilt the city's fortifications and encouraged his commanders to fight.

He set to work resolutely and built up all the wall
that was broken down, and raised towers on it . . .
He also made weapons and shields in abundance.
And he set combat commanders over the people,
and gathered them together to him in the square
at the gate of the city and spoke encouragingly to them,
saying, "Be strong and of good courage.
Do not be afraid or dismayed before the king of Assyria
and all the horde that is with him;
for there is one greater with us than with him.
With him is an arm of flesh;
but with us is the LORD our God, to help us
and to fight our battles." And the people took confidence
from the words of Hezekiah king of Judah.
2 Chronicles 32:5–8 (RSV)

Unfortunately, these valiant efforts were only partially successful. Jerusalem itself was spared, as Isaiah's chronicle later recounts. But Judah as a kingdom was largely lost. Over forty cities and towns were captured by the Assyrians. Judah's army collapsed. According to Sennacherib's own military campaign records, many of Judah's soldiers defected or ran, often abandoning their weapons as well as their defensive positions.

> All your rulers have fled together,
> without the bow they were captured.
> All of you who were found were captured,
> though they had fled far away.
> Isaiah 22:3 (RSV)

Isaiah was bitterly disappointed. Not only had the king not heeded his warnings, but now the people of Jerusalem who had survived the onslaught turned to self-indulgence, instead of mourning the catastrophic suffering of their fallen countrymen and the humiliating defeat of their army.

> What do you mean that you have gone up,
> all of you, to the housetops,
> you who are full of shoutings . . .
> Your slain are not slain with the sword or dead in battle . . .
> Isaiah 22:1–2 (RSV)

Isaiah's implication is that the shouts on the rooftops of Jerusalem were shouts of revelry, not of battle, that people were slain not by weapons but by drunken stupor. Instead of recognizing God's chastening hand and turning to repentance, they chose to "eat and drink" with fatalistic abandon, sealing their fate for a future reckoning.

In all fairness to the survivors of Jerusalem, their reaction is understandable. Their hopes had been raised, then crushed. They knew too well the fate of the fallen. Their times, after all, were more brutal than we can imagine. Elsewhere Isaiah himself describes the fate of the defeated:

> Whoever is found will be thrust through,
> and whoever is caught will fall by the sword.
> Their infants will be dashed in pieces before their eyes;
> their houses will be plundered and their wives ravished.
> Isaiah 13:15–16 (RSV)

These were hard times made all the worse by corrupt officials in Judah's own government. One of these in particular drew Isaiah's ire. Out of all the great figures of the era—kings, generals, priests, politicians, etc.—Isaiah singled out a civil servant named Shebna for a personalized prophetic rebuke. Shebna's name appears elsewhere in Isaiah (Isaiah 36:3) without the same condemnation, which has led some scholars to wonder if the two were the same man. But the real question is why Isaiah went after him in the first place.

According to the text, this Shebna was a self-important social climber, probably from an undistinguished family, who by commissioning an upper-class tomb for himself sought to memorialize his own significance. Isaiah personally appeared at Shebna's tomb site to pronounce the man's downfall.

> "What have you to do here . . .
> that you have hewn here a tomb for yourself,
> you who carve a tomb on the height . . .
> Behold, the Lord will hurl you away violently, O you strongman.
> He will seize firm hold on you, and whirl you round and round,
> and throw you like a ball into a wide land; there you shall die . . ."
> Isaiah 22:16–18 (RSV)

There must have been more to this story than we know to trigger such a vitriolic diatribe by such a renowned prophet. No doubt, the world then, as now, was full of Shebna-types manipulating their way to the top and then building minor monuments to themselves. So what made this Shebna distinct? Did he undermine Isaiah's activity or reputation, exploit a member of Isaiah's own family, or humiliate Isaiah publicly? Very probably this high government official was one of those who encouraged King Hezekiah to ally with Egypt in the futile revolt against Assyria, which Isaiah had opposed.

Ironically, Shebna does not seem to have suffered the fate which Isaiah prophesied. He did get demoted from "chief of staff" in the royal household to a kind of "secretary of state" position, but that was a minor shift in power. Eventually, of course, he did get "wrapped up tightly" (another reading for "whirled round and round") when in death he was wrapped in burial cloths and presumably laid to rest in the fancy tomb he had built.

But the interpersonal conflict here may be less important than what it tells us about Isaiah. Clearly, he was a man to be reckoned with, a man of influence, though often defeated politically. Isaiah was neither a shy nor a reticent man. He was intense, fearless, and fully attuned to the social and political happenings of his day. What must have made him downright scary at times to the people around him was that prophets of his time were often considered to be people whose words had special power. Oracles pronounced against foreign powers, as we see in these chapters, were the equivalent of religious weapons to be fired at various foes. In ancient Egypt, for example, curses were even etched into clay pots that were then shattered on the ground in a kind of sympathetic magic to weaken enemies.

Alternatively, one can understand prophets such as Isaiah as "religious secretaries of state," directly charged with representing divine input in international affairs. In the end, though, Isaiah was as human as the rest of us, fallible, emotional, wrestling with the events and personalities in his daily life. Still, if Shebna's story and Isaiah's reaction to the behavior of Jerusalem's citizens are any indication, one would not want to make him angry. He did, after all, have the last word.

For Discussion

1. Who are the Shebnas in your life—those who represent arrogance, opposition, or a manipulative disregard for others in their climb towards the top? How should you deal with them and with your own feelings about them?
2. Prophecy isn't always sequential. The passages in Isaiah's book jump around from time to time, event to event, monarch to monarch, sometimes combining prophecies written by Isaiah for one occasion with words added by his followers to apply to another situation. Isaiah's criticism of Jerusalem's people, for example, probably got linked to prophetic decrees over one hundred years later when Jerusalem actually fell to the Babylonians (e.g., Isaiah 20:4–11). Does that bother you? Is Isaiah's witness any less profound or Scripture's message less important if God uses multiple speakers to convey it? Do we sometimes run the risk of worshiping the text rather than the Author when we argue about how the text came to be?

For Reflection

What would you do if you knew that you would die tomorrow? Take a piece of paper and try to actually outline your coming hours and how you would spend them. Then stand back and review what you have composed.

What emerges as most important to you? What are you afraid of? What brings you comfort? What can you still create in the moments you have left? What message will you leave?

For Prayer

God of our joys, despair, conflicts, and peace, steer us through the ups and downs of each of our days, reassured by the promise of your steady presence and eternal purpose. Protect and heal us from the wounds inflicted by others, and forgive us for the wounds which we inflict ourselves. Implant in us a faith deeper than our anxieties so that whatever tomorrow brings, we face it not with fear but with hope. Amen.

30

Meaning

"O Lord, you are my God, I will extol you and praise your name;
For you have fulfilled your wonderful plans of old,
faithful and true."

ISAIAH 25:1 (NAB)

Originally created for a BBC radio broadcast, *The Hitchhiker's Guide to the Galaxy* by Douglas Adams is a zany science fiction series about earth, aliens, and the end of the universe. One of its main characters is an intimidating, condescending mega-computer named "Deep Thought." Deep Thought is tasked with finding the ultimate answer, the answer to "life, the universe, everything" (much to the chagrin of philosophers who protest that such inquiry is their domain alone—and which, if successful, would threaten their livelihood). After pondering the subject for several million years, Deep Thought finally acknowledges that the answer is beyond his computing capacity. However, Deep Thought prophesies the coming of another, greater computer (which he himself will design): "I speak of the computer that is to come after me . . . (whose) merest operational parameters I am not worthy to calculate." (Some readers will recognize in this quote a parody of John 1:27: "he who comes after me, the thong of whose sandal I am not worthy to untie.") The organic computer to come (that turns out to be planet Earth) will reveal the answer to "life, the universe, everything." In the end, the answer is indeed discovered, but it proves thoroughly unsatisfying, because it requires reformulating the original question.

Chapters 24–27 of the book of Isaiah, often misleadingly referred to as the "Apocalypse of Isaiah," also address the answer to "life, the universe, everything." These chapters, too, include references to earth, to the "hosts of heaven," and to the "universe" as Isaiah's people understood it. Altogether, these chapters interweave a complex tapestry of experiences and reflections accumulated over decades if not centuries by the people of the prophets. They include everything from fragments of war imagery (cities destroyed) to psalms of personal trust and national redemption, to a vivid description of earth's devastation under God's judgment.

Essentially, what Isaiah did for his own time—interpreting events, communicating God's intent, and helping his people to see the bigger picture of God's involvement in human history—his successors did for those who came after. From their experiences of war and suffering, from encounters with foreign nations to deliverance from seemingly hopeless situations, the theologians of God's people constructed a coherent explanation of how the pieces of God's great plan fit together. In an age without television, the internet, or modern print resources, the rich literature of the prophets became the defining source of information and understanding for personal meaning, for national identity, and for world events. The prophets and those like them wrote the narrative that shaped both the self-understanding and the future of God's people.

It worked! Israel's story outlasted the stories of far greater empires, from Egypt to Assyria to Babylon and beyond. Today it is Isaiah's voice that speaks to us across the centuries, not that of the Assyrians.

Doom and deliverance—these are the drumbeats of the prophetic rhythm:

> Behold, the Lord will lay waste the earth
> and make it desolate . . .
> The earth mourns and withers, the world languishes and withers;
> the heavens languish together with the earth.
> The earth lies polluted . . . a curse devours the earth
> and its inhabitants suffer for their guilt . . .
> The earth is utterly broken . . . violently shaken . . .
> the earth staggers like a drunken man, it sways like a hut.
> Isaiah 24:1, 4–6, 18–20 (RSV)

Prophets like Isaiah, Jeremiah, and Amos were convinced that there would be a day of reckoning for humanity's injustice and unfaithfulness. They saw the earth as "polluted" not as we understand it in terms of the

CO_2 or garbage we create today but by our accursed habit of mutual self-destruction. The murderous blood-letting in which humans have engaged since the days of Cain and Abel is a violation of Creation itself and of the covenant God established with humanity.

> For behold, the Lord is coming forth out of his place
> to punish the inhabitants of the earth for their iniquity,
> and the earth will disclose the blood shed upon her,
> and will no more cover her slain.
> Isaiah 26:21 (RSV)

All victims of war, genocide, and other kinds of violence will be accounted for, their pain and suffering revealed.

> And it shall be, as with the people, so with the priest;
> as with the maid, so with her mistress;
> as with the buyer, so with the seller;
> as with the lender, so with the borrower . . .
> Isaiah 24:2 (RSV)

God's calamitous judgment will not discriminate. Accountability will put us all in the same boat. Not even the powerful will escape.

> On that day the Lord will punish the host of heaven, in heaven,
> and the kings on earth, on the earth.
> They will be gathered together as prisoners in a pit . . .
> and after many days they will be punished.
> Isaiah 24:21–22 (RSV)

God's reckoning will be so complete as to nearly return earth to its primeval chaos. As happened when God cleansed earth's corruption in the story of Noah, the "windows of heaven" (Isaiah 24:18; Genesis 7:11–12) will open, and earth's very foundation will tremble. Intriguingly, the text of Isaiah employs a distinctive image to emphasize the point.

> The wine dries up, the vine languishes,
> all the merry-hearted sigh.
> The mirth of the timbrels is stilled,
> the noise of the jubilant has ceased . . .
> No longer do they drink wine with singing . . .
> There is an outcry in the streets for lack of wine;
> all joy has reached its eventide;
> the gladness of the earth is banished.
> Isaiah 24:7–11 (NRSV)

Throughout the book of Isaiah wine and feasting become the metaphor for happiness, the antithesis of judgment and destruction. True, drunkenness is associated with dissipation and downfall. But wine itself and the vineyards which produce it are consistently associated with God's presence and blessing.

Early in the book of Isaiah, for example, in the "Song of the Vineyard" (Isaiah 5:1–7), Judah and Israel are described as God's personal vineyard. After God's great judgment takes place, the vineyard which God had abandoned and destroyed comes back.

> In that day: "A pleasant vineyard, sing of it!
> I, the LORD, am its keeper; every moment I water it.
> Lest any one harm it, I guard it night and day . . ."
> Isaiah 27:2–3 (RSV)

One of the most remarkable texts in Isaiah features wine and feasting as the epitome of the deliverance and restoration of God's people.

> On this mountain the Lord of hosts
> will make for all peoples
> a feast of rich food, a feast of well-aged wines,
> of rich food filled with marrow,
> of well-aged wines strained clear.
> Isaiah 25:6 (NRSV)

This text, packed with meaning, illustrates the final deliverance and vindication of God's people and plan. As Moses and the elders of the Exodus gathered before God on Mt. Sinai (Exodus 24:9–11), so God's people will gather on God's holy mountain (presumably Mt. Zion) in the kind of royal banquet that includes what all feasts do: abundance, fellowship, and the joy God intends for humanity. In addition, this particular feast augers something more as well, something quite extraordinary.

> And he will destroy on this mountain the covering that is cast over
> all peoples,
> the veil that is spread over all nations.
> He will swallow up death for ever,
> and the LORD GOD will wipe away tears from all faces,
> and the reproach of his people he will take away from all the earth . . .
> Isaiah 25:7–8 (RSV)

Not only is this feast a spectacular vindication and restoration of Isaiah's people; it stresses God's intent to deliver all people and all nations not only from life's conflicts and suffering but from death itself. How amazing that after ten chapters of oracles against foreign nations, this picture of deliverance for all nations emerges. Initially, through Isaiah and other prophets a theology had developed to address the increasingly "global" context that they faced and how the people of Judah would be delivered from the multi-national maelstrom. Here, the understanding emerges that the deliverance itself will be global, not just vindicating God's work with the people of the covenant with Abraham but also with the people of the covenant with Noah which included all of humanity (Genesis 8:21).

Meanwhile, for the Hebrew people themselves the assurance of their own deliverance was affirmed in multiple ways.

> In that day this song will be sung in the land of Judah:
> "We have a strong city; he sets up salvation as walls and bulwarks.
> Open the gates, that the righteous nation
> which keeps faith may enter in."
> Isaiah 26:1–2 (RSV)

> In the days to come Jacob shall take root,
> Israel shall blossom and put forth shoots,
> and fill the whole world with fruit.
> Isaiah 27:6 (RSV)

Even ancient images from Canaanite and Babylonian mythologies, as well as from Hebrew tradition, are employed to convey God's triumphant deliverance.

> In that day the Lord with his hard and great and strong sword
> will punish Leviathan the fleeing serpent,
> Leviathan the twisting serpent,
> and he will slay the dragon that is in the sea.
> Isaiah 27:1 (RSV)

What more could even modern video game enthusiasts want than a story where the mighty sword of God slays the dragon of destruction?

In the end, however, only God can deliver, the prophets insisted. Our efforts invariably fall short.

> Like a woman with child,
> who writhes and cries out in her pangs,
> when she is near her time,
> so were we because of you, O Lord;
> we were with child, we writhed,

> but we gave birth only to wind.
> We have won no victories on earth . . .
> Isaiah 26:17–18a (NRSV)

But with God there is hope, peace, and justice.

> Trust in the Lord forever,
> for in the LORD GOD you have an everlasting rock . . .
> For when your judgments are in the earth,
> the inhabitants of the world learn righteousness . . .
> Those of steadfast mind you keep in peace—
> in peace because they trust in you.
> Isaiah 26:4, 9b, 3 (NRSV)

Isaiah would be glad that we are still reading these words.

For Discussion

1. It is impossible to list all the movies and books that portray earth's imminent destruction, whether via alien invasion, nuclear holocaust, meteor strikes, mutant creatures, or whatever. (Isaiah probably would have loved modern science fiction.) Why are we so fascinated with end-of-times imagery, with images of conflict, judgment, and destruction?

2. Some commentators say that in Isaiah 26:19 we see the earliest reference to resurrection in the Bible: "Your dead shall live, their corpses shall rise." Others say that this is a generalized reference to the rebirth of the nation of Judah (perhaps after the Babylonian Exile), not to individual resurrection. Still others see it as a literary device used in contrast to the preceding words in the same chapter which declare the destruction of God's enemies:

   > The dead do not live; shades do not rise—
   > because you have punished and destroyed them,
   > and wiped out all memory of them.
   > Isaiah 26:14 (NRSV)

   What is your belief about resurrection? Is it mainly a symbol of hope, a psychological outgrowth of the human experience of death and loss which finds expression in religions world-wide? Or is it a literal reality that will come for better or ill to each one of us? What shapes your view?

3. How should we understand God's feast on the mountain where the veil is lifted from "all nations" and "all peoples" and when God will wipe away the tears from "all faces"? Is this an image of universal salvation even while God's personal covenant relationship with a particular people is reaffirmed ("the reproach of his people he will take away from all the earth"—Isaiah 25:8)?

   For Christians this can be a particularly vexing question. For centuries Christian missions have often been driven by the conviction that an exclusive confession of Jesus as Lord is the key to personal salvation. However, there have also always been in Scripture and church teaching from the very beginning more inclusive ways of understanding God's grace. In the modern world where people of different faiths interact as never before in human history, views are shifting significantly. Where do you stand? Who do you think will be seated at God's feast on the mountain?

For Reflection

Go to the mountain, dressed for the feast. Join the streaming crowds, gathering for the most fabulous meal ever prepared. Imagine yourself seated at the banquet, sipping exquisite wine, surrounded by ecstatic people from every land and time. Feel your eyes widen and pulse quicken and breath catch when the divine host abruptly announces the end of all sorrow, the promise that all of life's suffering and loss will cease forever. Look at the wonder, the relief, the disbelief in the faces around you. What does it feel like to finally be free?

For Prayer

Righteous Deliverer, transform our tears into the glistening dew of a new day, full of promise. Through us spread the news of the coming feast, the invitation to all peoples and nations to meet at the mountain of deliverance where all truth will be revealed and all sorrows erased. Fill our cups with the wine of renewal that together we may taste of true grace and give you thanks. Amen.

31

Drink Up

"The meek shall obtain fresh joy in the LORD"

ISAIAH 29:19A (NRSV)

AS A YOUNG TEACHER in Japan I imbibed in the local culture, which is to say I became a member of a local bar where a person could buy a bottle of one's favorite liquor that was then stamped with the club customer's name and kept in a rack for the next visit. That way, by the time the customer came in and sat down, one's favorite drink was already poured and waiting. On Friday nights, after the usual fifty-some hours of classes per week, having one's own *Cheers*-friendly watering hole was a very pleasant way to unwind.

One Friday evening, however, upon arriving late for the weekly retreat, I ended up on a bar stool at a crowded counter next to a clearly inebriated older gentleman who was hunched alone over his drink. After muttering angrily into his glass for some time, the man suddenly spun his stool towards me, leaned forward with boozy breath and sputtered into my face, "You killed my father. You killed my uncle . . . and my cousin."

Needless to say, this was an unexpected and discomforting salutation. But it initiated a moving conversation about World War II and the losses this man's family had endured, the pain of which he was clearly still trying to numb after all these years. Being the first American he had ever met, I became the natural receptacle for the words he had needed to pour out for more than three decades. Once released, different words could follow, words of sorrow, consolation, and a measure of reconciliation. A few drinks later the conversation closed with an awkward embrace and the pained but hopeful words, "I didn't know Americans could be human."

> Woe to the proud crown of the drunkards of Ephraim . . .
> which is on the head of the rich valley
> of those overcome with wine!
> Isaiah 28:1 (RSV)

The proud "drunkards of Ephraim" were human, too. We forget that when we read the texts of Isaiah. What we have before us in this book is the product of centuries of refinement: the original, authentic words of the great prophet Isaiah set in a composition rich with the insights of his followers as they applied his teachings to other situations as well. But behind this extraordinary work were the lives of real people, including the people of Ephraim, about whom we hear in this text only because they were on the receiving end of one of Isaiah's diatribes. But the people of Ephraim had their own story to tell.

At the time of Isaiah's prophecy about them (around 725 BCE) the people of Ephraim were all that was left of the alliance against Assyria which Isaiah had warned King Ahaz about. Assyria had crushed their supporters in Damascus a decade earlier and now, Isaiah warned, their own demise would soon be complete.

> Behold, the Lord has one who is mighty and strong . . .
> he will cast down to the earth with violence.
> The proud crown of the drunkards of Ephraim
> will be trodden under foot . . .
> Isaiah 28:2–3 (RSV)

No wonder they were drinking! But their dismal future was not Isaiah's primary concern. Rather, it was the future of his own people in Judah two decades later who were facing the same threat.

> These also reel with wine and stagger with strong drink;
> the priest and the prophet reel with strong drink,
> they are confused with wine, they stagger with strong drink;
> they err in vision, they stumble in giving judgment.
> For all tables are full of vomit, no place is without filthiness.
> Isaiah 28:7–8 (RSV)

Does Isaiah's graphic commentary indicate that Isaiah had an issue with alcohol? Or had he simply run out of other vices to condemn? After all, he had already railed against social injustice, self-indulgent fashion, the court system, political corruption, religious abuses, and so on. In a pre-video, pre-cocaine, pre-Wall Street and K Street society, his options were more limited than they would be today.

Alcohol, nonetheless, was not the issue. What triggered Isaiah's ire was the delusional thinking of Judah's political leaders, who were once again plotting against Assyria. Isaiah had seen it before. The last time God's people had staged such a rebellion, they had not only been crushed, but many of the people of the northern kingdom of Israel had been physically deported while their country was destroyed. Now, at the time of Isaiah's latest prophecy nearly twenty years later (around 703 BCE), history was repeating itself.

Isaiah's use of alcoholic stupor imagery was his way of shouting, "What are you thinking?!" The lessons of the northern kingdom (and the people of Ephraim) were part of living memory, a case study in stupidity within Judah's own faith family. Could they not see the parallels? The stupor Isaiah described was not just chemical. This time it was political and religious as well.

For the leaders of Judah, however, including King Hezekiah, politics trumped prophecy. These were, after all, heady times. Sargon, the Assyrian king who had conquered the northern kingdom had just died and his successor, Sennacherib, was tied up with revolts on the other side of the empire. Hezekiah had rebuilt Judah's defenses and strengthened its military. Alliances with Egypt and other rebel powers were in the works. Emissaries crisscrossed the region just as we see on television today when envoys from capitols such as Washington, DC or London journey to cities such as Jerusalem, Baghdad, Cairo, or Kabul. In this moment of national confidence, Judah saw an opportunity to exploit Assyrian weaknesses. Isaiah disapproved, mocking the doomed endeavors.

> An oracle on the beasts of the Negeb.
> [the desert route between Jerusalem and Egypt]
> Through a land of trouble and anguish . . .
> they carry their riches on the backs of asses
> and their treasures [e.g., bribes] on the humps of camels,
> to a people who cannot profit them.
> For Egypt's help is worthless and empty,
> therefore I have called her "Rahab who sits still."
> Isaiah 30:6–7 (RSV)

Isaiah's acid wit comes through in comparing Egypt to Rahab, Rahab being another name for a monster of chaos. Already in Isaiah's time Egypt was famous for its sphinx sculptures with the face of a human on an animal's body. Like a sphinx, Isaiah implies, Rahab (Egypt) "sits still," a powerless monster, stuck in the sand.

Isaiah met stiff opposition. His was apparently a singular voice in the royal court; he was an unpopular prophet with a minority view. The religious establishment clearly supported the national policy of military solutions to political problems.

Some think that Isaiah's diatribe against the drunken priests and prophets may reflect an actual occasion, perhaps a kind of "state dinner," celebrating (with considerable abandon, apparently) the signing of a mutual defense pact with Egypt. In their favor, the advocates of nationalism had history on their side. After all, God had delivered their people from slavery in Egypt and helped them conquer their way into the Promised Land. God had defeated their enemies before, from the Philistines to the recent alliance of their northern neighbors against them. There were even many in Isaiah's day who believed that God would never allow Jerusalem, God's holy city, to fall. Numerous passages in Isaiah illustrate that view.

> But the multitude of your foes shall be like small dust,
> and the multitude of the ruthless like passing chaff.
> And in an instant, suddenly, you will be visited
> by the LORD of hosts . . .
> And the multitude of all the nations
> that fight against Ariel [Jerusalem],
> all that fight against her and her stronghold and distress her,
> shall be like a dream, a vision of the night . . .
> so shall the multitude of all the nations be
> that fight against Mount Zion.
> Isaiah 29:5–6a, 78c (RSV)

> Like birds hovering,
> so the Lord of hosts will protect Jerusalem;
> he will protect and deliver it, he will spare and rescue it.
> Isaiah 31:5 (RSV)

Whether or not Isaiah himself held this view is a matter of debate, though he certainly did later declare that Jerusalem would survive Sennacherib's siege. In the meantime, Isaiah was an outcast. At a time when it was politically popular and even patriotic for religious leaders to support national ambitions, Isaiah stood firmly opposed to them. To register his resistance Isaiah ensured that his views were recorded.

> Go now, write it before them on a tablet,
> and inscribe it in a book,
> so that it may be for the time to come as a witness for ever.
> For they are a rebellious people, faithless children,
> children who will not hear the instruction of the LORD;
> who say to the seers, "Do not see";
> and to the prophets, "Do not prophesy to us what is right;
> speak to us smooth things, prophesy illusions,
> leave the way, turn aside from the path,
> let us hear no more about the Holy One of Israel."
> Isaiah 30:8–11 (NRSV)

Ultimately, Isaiah prevailed. As he expected, later generations witnessed the tragic outcome of the religious and political stupor against which Isaiah had railed. Eventually, after Sennacherib's armies had devastated Judah and defeated Egypt, it was Isaiah to whom King Hezekiah turned for guidance, not the foolish, fawning priests and politicians who had dug the nation into such a hole. More than anyone in biblical history, Isaiah could qualify as the patron saint of "I told you so."

Certainly, it is Isaiah's account that we go by today. The drunkards of Ephraim and those drunk with power, ambition and religious delusion in Isaiah's Jerusalem paid the price for not heeding his words. Like us, they were merely human, with all the faults which that implies, including a capacity for bad choices, self-delusion, and interpersonal conflict. But Isaiah was human, too, and through his humanity God was addressing these people with words of warning and promise to lead them away from disaster towards the hopeful future that God intends for all who are created human.

We can each help shape that future ourselves every day by the choices we make, the words we heed, and the way we respond, even in chance encounters.

For Discussion

1. "Speak to us of smooth things . . . let us hear no more of the Holy One of Israel" (Isaiah 30:10–11). Does Isaiah's caricature of his contemporaries ring true for you? Do you sometimes get tired of the life of faith and long for smoother alternatives? When does faith make life smoother and when does it not?
2. By the time of his confrontation with the drunken priests, Isaiah could have been in his fifties, already established and esteemed after three decades of service as a prophet for his people. Yet his own people, public leaders, and the religious elite rejected his counsel. Have you ever been at odds with religious leaders in your own faith community, with decision-makers, or with fellow worshipers? How does that feel? Is it worse than conflicts at work or in the political sphere? Isaiah became angry and bitter, at least for a while. Did you?

Most of us will never be an Isaiah, speaking directly for God. Nor does being in the minority make one right. Nevertheless, how do we find our way through conflicts with fellow believers in ways consistent with the faith we proclaim?

For Reflection

> The Lord said:
> "Because this people draw near with their mouth
> and honor me with their lips,
> while their hearts are far from me,
> and their worship of me is a commandment of men
> learned by rote;
> so will I again do amazing things with this people,
> shocking and amazing.
> The wisdom of their wise shall perish,
> and the discernment of the discerning shall be hidden."
> Isaiah 29:13–14 (RSV)

How much of our religion today is merely "a commandment of men learned by rote?" Consider God's amazing response to that: "Therefore, behold, I will again do marvelous things with this people, wonderful and marvelous." Fully knowing that our hearts are "far from" God, God chooses to do something unexpected, to recreate the future in order to move us from rote religion to living faith. Does this inversion of conventional (human) wisdom give you hope? Can you identify something marvelous or wonderful in your own faith journey that has refreshed your spirit?

For Prayer

Lord of new possibilities, draw our hearts closer to you. Guide us in the conflicts and turmoils of life, especially with those close to us. Make our "humanity" a gift we can offer to all who are wounded or in need of comfort or simply seeking company for sharing life's joys. Open us to all that is wonderful, marvelous, and a testimony to your love and grace. Amen.

32

The Bigger They Are . . .

"I have heard a decree of destruction from the Lord God of hosts upon the whole land."

ISAIAH 28:22B (NRSV)

No one has ever accused Isaiah of mincing words. Like all great orators he had a gift for metaphor. On top of that, Isaiah exhibited an exceptional talent for sarcasm.

> Therefore hear the word of the Lord,
> you scoffers who rule this people in Jerusalem . . . you have said,
> "We have made a covenant with death, and with
> Sheol we have an agreement;
> when the overwhelming scourge passes through
> it will not come to us; for we have made lies our refuge,
> and in falsehood we have taken shelter . . ."
> Isaiah 28:14–15 (NRSV)

Clearly, the leaders of Jerusalem would not have described themselves as being protected by lies or committed to a covenant with death. But scoffing the ones he called scoffers, Isaiah dared to call their political pact with Egypt exactly such a bargain.

> "Woe to the rebellious children," says the Lord,
> "who carry out a plan,
> but not mine; and who make a league, but not of my spirit . . .
> who set out to go down to Egypt, without asking for my counsel,
> to take refuge in the protection of Pharaoh,
> and to seek shelter in the shadow of Egypt!"
> Isaiah 30:1–2 (RSV)

Sheol was the Hebrew realm of the dead. *Moth,* the Hebrew word used here by Isaiah to mean death, was derived from the name for the ancient Canaanite God of death and infertility. In Egypt's famed cult of the dead, gods such as Osiris were also associated with the underworld. "To make a league, but not of my spirit" was God's way via Isaiah of stating that the political agreement between Judah and Egypt was a suicidal compact. Worse, the agreement was idolatrous because it was probably sealed by the Egyptians in the name of their gods, something which prophets such as Isaiah condemned as capitulating to false gods.

> Your covenant with death will be annulled,
> and your agreement with Sheol will not stand;
> when the overwhelming scourge passes through
> you will be beaten down by it.
> As often as it passes through it will take you . . .
> and it will be sheer terror . . .
> Isaiah 28:18–19 (RSV)

Words such as these make it easy for us to understand why Isaiah might have received a less than hospitable reception at the royal court and among the religious establishment. Isaiah even recorded their indignant response.

> "Whom will he teach knowledge,
> and to whom will he explain the message?
> Those who are weaned from the milk, those taken from the breast?
> For it is precept upon precept, precept upon precept,
> line upon line, line upon line, here a little, there a little."
> Isaiah 28:9–10 (RSV)

In this delightfully wicked quotation of their own derision of him, Isaiah makes fun of his accusers. "Who does he think we are?" Isaiah imitates, "Children? He just prattles nonsense." In the Hebrew text Isaiah uses un-translatable alliteration to mimic their criticism of him, making their remarks sound like school children bickering: "Precept upon precept, line upon line, here a little, there a little . . ." to which Isaiah essentially responds, "If you won't listen to me, you will get another, tougher teacher."

> By men of strange lips and with an alien tongue
> [the Assyrians]
> the Lord will speak to his people . . .
> Therefore the word of the Lord will be to
> *them* precept upon precept . . . line upon line . . .

that they may go, and fall backward, and be broken,
and snared, and taken.
Isaiah 28:11, 13 (RSV, italics added)

Isaiah goes on to tell them that the Lord will rise up as he did for David and Joshua (Isaiah 28:21), coming in storm and fury to "work his work—alien is his work" (28:21). In fact, God will do something utterly unexpected, namely, fighting against his own people in order to teach them a lesson.

"Behold, I am laying in Zion for a foundation a stone,
a tested stone,
a precious cornerstone, of a sure foundation . . .
And I will make justice the line,
and righteousness the plummet . . ."
Isaiah 28:16–17a (RSV)

The kind of stone referred to by Isaiah is a hard stone, good for engraving and thus for using as a standard for cutting other stones to size. Through the centuries the cornerstone mentioned here has been interpreted as referring to everything from Solomon's temple to the Davidic monarchy to the righteous remnant to the Messiah. At the very least, it was God's way of measuring Judah's alliance with Egypt as a failure.

The Egyptians are human, and not God;
their horses are flesh, and not spirit.
When the LORD stretches out his hand, the helper will stumble,
and the one helped will fall, and they will all perish together.
Isaiah 31:3 (NRSV)

The decision-makers in Jerusalem thought they were making a clever political move. But Isaiah warned that "the wisdom of their wise shall perish" (Isaiah 29:14b). God is wise, too, Isaiah countered, wise enough in fact to thwart them.

Woe to those who . . . do not look to the Holy One of Israel
or consult the Lord!
And yet he is wise and brings disaster,
he does not call back his words,
but will arise against the house of evildoers,
and against the helpers of those who work iniquity.
Isaiah 31:1–2 (RSV)

If there is any comfort for Isaiah's audience, both on this occasion and throughout the years that followed, it was in the prophecies that Assyria, too, like Egypt, would eventually fall in accordance with God's greater plan.

> "Then the Assyrian shall fall by a sword, not of mortals;
> and a sword, not of humans, shall devour him;
> he shall flee from the sword,
> and his young men shall be put to forced labor."
> Isaiah 31:8 (NRSV)

It took another hundred years before Babylonia finally ousted Assyria as the region's dominant new empire. Before Babylonia became Judah's new oppressor, finally destroying Jerusalem itself in 587 BCE, Isaiah's people had time to reflect on Isaiah's prophecies and on how Jerusalem had survived the Assyrian siege in 701 BCE. Later writers took Isaiah's own words to describe Assyria's demise.

> Behold, the name of the Lord comes from far,
> burning with his anger, and in thick rising smoke . . .
> his breath is like an overflowing stream that reaches up to the neck;
> to sift the nations with the sieve of destruction . . .
> And the Lord will cause his majestic voice to be heard
> and the descending blow of his arm to be seen, in furious anger
> and a flame of devouring fire,
> with a cloudburst and tempest and hailstones.
> The Assyrians will be terror-stricken at the voice of the LORD,
> when he smites with his rod . . .
> [and] every stroke of the staff of punishment . . .
> Isaiah 30:27a, 28, 30–31 (RSV)

In his early years when counseling King Ahaz, Isaiah had referred to Assyria as a river about to flood Judah up to its neck (Isaiah 8:7). Now, says Isaiah, it is God who will overflow Assyria up to its neck. Previously, Isaiah had described Assyria as a rod used by God, "the rod of my anger, the staff of my fury" (Isaiah 10:5) against Judah. Now it is Assyria that the Lord will strike with a rod of punishment. As Isaiah had often described God's coming in fury and fire to judge the nations, including Judah, now God would burn Assyria on the garbage pit of history, symbolized by both the smoldering garbage dump called *Topheth* outside of Jerusalem's city walls and also by comparing Assyria to Molech whose victims were consigned to fire.

> For a burning place [*Topheth*] has long been prepared;
> Yea, for the *Molech* it is made ready, its pyre made deep and wide,
> with fire and wood in abundance;
> the breath of the Lord, like a stream of brimstone, kindles it.
> Isaiah 30:33 (RSV)

After nearly a century of Assyrian oppression, the hostility conveyed in these images is understandable. Isaiah had done his best to warn his people against the danger that was coming, calling them to focus on God's help, not Egypt's. After Isaiah, the people of Jerusalem had to live with Assyria's boot on their neck for decades. Could it have turned out differently? Isaiah thought so.

For Discussion

1. "God has a plan for your life" is a phrase we hear often. "Woe to the rebellious children," says the Lord, "who carry out a plan, but not mine" (Isaiah 30:1a, RSV). How do we find out what God's plan is and whether or not our lives and the life of our community are in harmony with it?

> Stupefy yourselves and be in a stupor,
> blind yourselves and be blind!
> Be drunk but not with wine; stagger, but not with strong drink!
> For the Lord has poured out upon you a spirit of deep sleep,
> and has closed your eyes, the prophets,
> and covered your heads, the seers.
> Isaiah 29:9–11a (RSV)

2. We sometimes say "There are none so blind as those who will not see." Does God sometimes actually block our understanding? Or, do our stubborn choices and irrational attachments accumulate to the point where we lose the capacity to see objectively?

For Reflection

"And the vision of all this has become to you like the words of a book that is sealed" (Isaiah 29:11a, RSV). Isaiah's ministry began with a vision. It sustained him for life, directed his labors, pitted him against his community, and helped him to see what even kings and religious leaders could not. How is your vision these days? Is it sealed shut or still open? What has it brought you in life? How has it changed over time? Try sketching your vision on paper—a vision map that outlines the continents of your belief, the peaks, valleys, and rivers of your journey across it, the towns, events, and encounters that altered your direction. What do you see beyond where you've been?

For Prayer

Governing God, nations rise, proliferate, and expire under your sovereign gaze. Yet your promises and people remain. Open our minds to a grander vision of reality. Help us to discern the signs and to heed the messages that will steer us not only towards truth but also towards faith, wisdom, and peace with life's unfolding design. Amen.

33

Zen Prophecy

"Therefore the Lord waits to be gracious to you . . ."

ISAIAH 30:18A (RSV)

ZAZEN IS THE WELL-KNOWN form of Japanese Buddhist meditation whereby one sits in a lotus-like posture, legs crossed, hands resting palms upwards on one's lap, eyes nearly closed. By focusing on something like breathing, counting, a mental enigma, or even an object such as a burning candle, one attempts to clear one's mind, to peel back the layers of daily distractions towards a mind open to a sudden spark of enlightenment.

Kyudo, or Zen archery, is a more active way of pursuing the same end, a disciplined approach to mental clarity. In Kyudo the archer concentrates not on the target but on the process of joining bow, arrow, and aim under a master's discipline, setting ego aside. The target becomes less an object of endeavor than a mirror of one's inner consciousness.

> For thus said the Lord God, the Holy One of Israel,
> "In returning and rest you shall be saved;
> in quietness and in trust shall be your strength."
> Isaiah 30:15 (RSV)

It is as though Isaiah were intoning: "Rest from all your restless plotting. Security will come not through striving but from yielding. Deliverance begins by opening oneself to a reality beyond immediate perception, by returning to the One who is the transcendent Reality."

In a situation of national turmoil, where the people of Judah were under attack by an invading army, internally divided, facing possible destruction and death, the prophet Isaiah conveyed an almost Zen-like call to calm. That message did not persuade Isaiah's audience at the time, and it is not an approach which most of us today would adopt either in similar circumstances. Yet there it is in the middle of all the prophetic diatribes and political conflicts: the counsel to "stop fighting it," to let go of anxieties over circumstances which the people could not control and to turn instead to complete trust in God's providence. "Turn to him from whom you have deeply revolted, O people of Israel" (Isaiah 31:6, RSV).

But would a passive response to an oppressive regime such as the Assyrians have worked? Could the people of Judah have ended up any worse off than they did, first as vassals to the Assyrian Empire and eventually as slaves of the Babylonians? We will never know. What we do know with certainty is that Isaiah's people said, "No" to God's offer.

> The Lord will speak to this people, to whom he has said,
> "This is rest; give rest to the weary; and this is repose;"
> yet they would not hear.
> Isaiah 28:11b–12 (RSV)

> And you would not, but you said,
> "No! We will speed upon horses,"
> therefore you shall speed away;
> and, "We will ride upon swift steeds,"
> therefore your pursuers shall be swift.
> Isaiah 30:15c, 16 (RSV)

They ran. But they could not hide. They stood out "like a flagstaff on the top of a mountain, like a signal on a hill" (Isaiah 30:17b), and were picked off accordingly.

Time and time again in Isaiah there is this contrast between obedience (or lack thereof) and consequence, between choice and punishment. In a way, the composers of the book of Isaiah were masters of the "good cop, bad cop" routine (as was Isaiah himself). In case after case, warnings of disaster are followed by reassurances of grace.

> The proud crown of the drunkards of Ephraim
> will be trodden under foot;
> and the fading flower of its glorious beauty . . .
> will be like a first-ripe fig before the summer;
> when a man sees it, he eats it up as soon as it is in his hand.
> Isaiah 28:3–4 (RSV)

But as soon as this declaration of devouring defeat is issued, there follows an image of deliverance, using some of the very same words ("crown" and "beauty"), turning the language of derision into language of hope.

> In that day the Lord of hosts will be a crown of glory,
> and a diadem of beauty, to the remnant of his people;
> and a spirit of justice to him who sits in judgment.
> Isaiah 28:5–6a (RSV)

Speaking of Jerusalem, Isaiah slips in an almost unnoticeable threat, amplifies it, then turns it around completely. "Ho Ariel, Ariel, the city where David encamped!" (Isaiah 29:1a, RSV). As Isaiah and his audience knew full well, David did not just "encamp" at Jerusalem. He besieged and conquered the city, taking it away from its original inhabitants, the Jebusites. That is how it became a Hebrew city in the first place. In the same way, Isaiah says, God "will encamp against you round about, and will besiege you with towers and I will raise siege works against you" (Isaiah 29:3, RSV).

This is not just a description of the Assyrian assault on Jerusalem in 701 BCE. It is the bad-cop God announcing judgment. But then things turn completely around: "you will be visited by the Lord of hosts . . . And the multitude of the nations that fight against Ariel (Isaiah 29:7a)" shall be "like small dust" (Isaiah 29:5a), just a dream (Isaiah 29:7).

In one of Isaiah's distinctive "Woe" pronouncements he lambastes the plotters of Hezekiah's court who made secret deals with Egypt in their revolt against Assyria.

> Woe to those who hide deep from the Lord their counsel,
> whose deeds are in the dark, and who say,
> "Who sees us? Who knows us?"
> You turn things upside down!
> Shall the potter be regarded as the clay;
> that the thing made should say of its maker,
> "He did not make me";
> or the thing formed say of him who formed it,
> "He has no understanding"?
> Isaiah 29:15–16 (RSV)

Isaiah even compares Judah's leaders to the ignorant and the illiterate.

> And the vision of all this has become to you
> like the words of a book that is sealed.
> When men give it to one who can read, saying, "Read this," he says,
> "I cannot, for it is sealed."
> And when they give the book to one who
> cannot read, saying, "Read this," he says, "I cannot read."
> Isaiah 29:11–12 (RSV)

But in the verses that follow comes an extraordinary promise of an idyllic day ahead:

On that day the deaf shall hear the words of a scroll,
and out of their gloom and darkness the eyes of the blind shall see.
The meek shall obtain fresh joy in the LORD,
and the neediest people
shall exalt in the Holy One of Israel.
For the tyrant shall be no more, and the scoffer cease to be;
and all those alert to do evil will be cut off . . .
Isaiah 29:18–20 (NRSV)

"Jacob shall no more be ashamed . . .
For when he sees his children,
the work of my hands, in his midst,
they will sanctify my name;
they will sanctify the Holy One of Jacob;
and will stand in awe of the God of Israel.
And those who err in spirit will come to understanding,
and those who murmur will accept instruction."
Isaiah 29:22–24 (RSV)

Isaiah's "good cop, bad cop" technique was evident even in what was probably one of his earlier prophecies, where Isaiah addressed the women of Judah, warning them of approaching danger.

Rise up, you women who are at ease, hear my voice;
you complacent daughters, give ear to my speech.
In little more than a year you will shudder, you complacent women;
for the vintage will fail, the fruit harvest will not come.
Tremble, you women who are at ease . . .
Isaiah 32:9–11 (RSV)

But then in the same context comes one of the most spectacular deliverance prophecies in scripture, saying that the suffering will continue only "until the Spirit is poured upon us from on high" (Isaiah 32:15a, RSV), bringing prosperity, justice, and peace. Later writers described this golden day in terms of a righteous kingdom where security and good sense would prevail.

Behold, a king will reign in righteousness,
and princes will rule in justice.
Each will be like a hiding place from the wind,
a covert from the tempest,
like streams of water in a dry place,
like the shade of a great rock in a weary land.
Then the eyes of those who see will not be closed,

and the ears of those who hear will hearken.
The mind of the rash will have good judgment,
and the tongue of the stammerers will speak readily and distinctly.
Isaiah 32:1–4 (RSV)

Perhaps one of the most flowery descriptions of all in the "good cop, bad cop" pattern came from someone who was probably able to look back generations later and confirm that what Isaiah had prophesied would surely come to pass.

Yea, O people of Zion who dwell at Jerusalem;
you will weep no more.
He will surely be gracious to you at the sound of your cry;
when he hears it, he will answer you.
And though the Lord give you the bread of adversity
and the water of affliction,
yet your Teacher will not hide himself anymore . . .
And he will give rain for the seed with which you sow the ground,
and grain, the produce of the ground,
which will be rich and plenteous . . .
And upon every lofty mountain
and high hill there will be brooks running with water . . .
Moreover the light of the moon will be as the light of the sun,
And the light of the sun will be sevenfold,
as the light of seven days,
in the day when the Lord binds up the hurt of his people,
and heals the wounds inflicted by his blow . . .
You shall have a song . . . and gladness of heart . . .
Isaiah 30:19–20, 23, 25a, 26 (RSV)

In this grand vision the cosmos itself is reconfigured to mirror the original seven days of creation and the restoration of creation's original bliss. How much more "good cop" can one get?

Even though Isaiah's "bad cop" messages were initially rejected, his visionary, "good-cop" promises became embedded in biblical faith. His images of a time of peace, prosperity, and justice in a society where life is fair, secure, and abundant have been inspiring people for two and a half millennia. They appeal to us still. But Isaiah would insist, today as much as ever, that the source of such life does not reside within human ambition. Zen Master Isaiah would direct us to resting in another Source, yielding to the reality and power of an enlightenment from beyond: the Holy One we call God.

For Discussion

1. The "good-cop, bad-cop" pattern of Isaiah was intended to motivate people to respond to God's message. What works for you? Do you need both promise and threat?
2. "Promise and Threat" seems to be a pattern embedded in everything from parenting to teaching to government. Why do you think that is? Are we simply evolutionary life-forms continually adapting to danger and gratification? Are we puppets of a divine being, treated like dependent children in need of training? Or, might we be part of a transformational cosmic journey that moves us from one kind of existence into another, as signaled by the words of the writer to the Ephesians in the New Testament?

   > Put off your old nature which belongs
   > to your former manner of life
   > and is corrupt through deceitful lusts,
   > and be renewed in the spirit of your minds,
   > and put on the new nature, created after the likeness of God
   > in true righteousness and holiness.
   > Ephesians 4:22–24 (RSV)

For Reflection

Meditate. If you've never tried Zazen, look it up on the internet; get a book from the library; rent or buy or download a video. Try a contemplative yoga posture. If you already use such techniques, try a familiar prayer posture: kneeling with hands raised, palm to palm, or sitting, head bowed, eyes shut, hands still or fingering beads. Sway, pray, repeat a phrase from Scripture (even Isaiah) or from your own faith tradition. Let yourself step away from daily striving and allow your busy mind to rest. See what comes when quiet, open space is created in your soul.

For Prayer

Waiting God, be patient with our restless striving. Remind us of the possibilities of peace. Hold before us the vision of the life you would have us enjoy where justice and security prevail, where our labors yield fruit that is satisfying to both body and soul, and where at all levels of our being we finally perceive in all its splendor the transcendent reality of which we are all a part. Amen.

34

The Rabshakeh

"Save us from his hand,
that all the kingdoms of the earth may know
that thou alone art the Lord."

ISAIAH 37:20 (RSV)

When my two Israeli friends opened their backpacks and took out a submachine gun and an old Smith & Wesson pistol, I knew that there was going to be more to the hike we were about to take than what they had told me. As their army buddies maneuvered the military jeep in which we were riding through the back streets of Jerusalem towards the edge of the city, my friends explained that we were going to hike the entire twenty-or-so miles across the barren Wilderness of Judaea with its three-thousand foot drop to the Dead Sea by sundown.

Why the guns and why the rush? As they loaded and checked their weapons, my fellow kibbutzniks calmly informed me that we were entering a restricted military area without permission, that it was being used for artillery practice (though their friend on active duty had phoned them the night before to say that this day the area wasn't scheduled to be a target zone), and that the army had increased patrols in the area due to recent infiltration activity by armed guerrillas.

Young, foolhardy, and already too far into the adventure to back out, I grabbed my backpack and sleeping bag when we were dropped off and followed my friends into the wadi at the edge of the desert. I thought the grueling pace would slack off once we were well into the barren, ravine-carved landscape, but we scrambled over rocks and rises and down steep slopes for several hours before finally resting at the remains of one of King Herod's likely winter retreats, traceable by the water channels etched into the rocky hillsides.

Not until late in the afternoon while crossing a small open expanse were we spotted and chased down by a truckload of Israeli soldiers. They approached us head-on, braking directly in front of the lead man in our single file of three (my friends had thoughtfully put me between them, since they were armed and I was not, and by this time we were spaced nearly ten yards apart—which, it turned out, was a good thing).

Having the guns of twenty-some soldiers trained directly upon us was, eerily, not all that frightening, although the large machine gun mounted on the cab of the truck and pointed at us by a tense young soldier gripping the trigger frame was definitely disconcerting. Not until five years later, on a second visit to Israel, did I learn that the commander yelling at us in Hebrew that day was saying that we were lucky not to have been shot on sight. We got off with an order to march north from where we were standing while they pursued another objective. Plus, we were notified that we would all be court-martialed, which would have been tricky, given that even though I was wearing military fatigues like my colleagues, was bearded and tanned like many soldiers, and was marching with two battle-tested veterans known to one of the troops in the truck (our "insider"), I wasn't even an Israeli citizen, much less in the army. But since the commander only spoke to the first guy in line, that never came out.

Did we march out as told and get court-martialed? Of course not. After heading in the direction ordered until the truck was out of sight, my friends suddenly bolted off the trail at a right angle and headed for a ravine, yelling at me to run with them. For several hours we played hide and seek with an army Jeep patrol, hiding behind boulders and sneaking through small wadis until clambering down the final descent to the Dead Sea where we hid for the night in a tall patch of rushes. Early the next morning we hiked out along the Dead Sea shoreline, again passing through restricted territory. As to the court-martial part, that got worked out privately by a sympathetic officer-friend who out-ranked the officer who caught us. But by that time I had already left the country.

> In the fourteenth year of King Hezekiah,
> Sennacherib king of Assyria came up
> against all the fortified cities of Judah
> and took them. And the king of Assyria

> sent the Rabshakeh from Lachish
> to King Hezekiah at Jerusalem, with a great army . . .
> Then the Rabshakeh stood and called out in a loud voice
> in the language of Judah:
> "Hear the words of the great king, the king of Assyria!
> Thus says the
> king: 'Do not let Hezekiah deceive you,
> for he will not be able to deliver you . . .
> Make your peace with me and come out to me . . .
> until I come and take you away . . .'"
> Isaiah 36:1–2, 13–14, 16a, 17a (RSV)

Hezekiah's "chief of staff," "secretary of state," and a court recorder had been dispatched to face the Assyrian envoy to hear his terms. In response to his ultimatum they replied,

> "Pray, speak to your servants in Aramaic, for we understand it;
> do not speak to us in the language of Judah within the
> hearing of the people who are on the wall."
> But the Rabshakeh said,
> "Has my master sent me to speak these words
> to your master and to you, and not to the men sitting on the wall,
> who are doomed with you to eat their own dung
> and drink their own urine?"
> Isaiah 36:11–12 (RSV)

Aramaic was the language of diplomacy and commerce in those days, while Hebrew was the language of the common people of Judah. Hezekiah's diplomats were trying to manage the threat level, all too aware that many fighters in Judah's army had already deserted in the face of such overwhelming odds. But the multi-lingual Rabshakeh put them at a tactical disadvantage.

One can almost picture the desperate scene, not unlike the siege of the city "Minas Tirith" in the Tolkien-based movie *The Lord of the Rings: The Return of the King*. There, the beleaguered king, his motley army, and the frightened citizens of the city are completely surrounded, facing imminent destruction by a terrible foe. At the last moment they are saved by the arrival of the white-clad, angel-like Gandalf, the good wizard, leading reinforcements. Perhaps not coincidentally, an angel appears in the Isaiah version, too, to slaughter the enemies and save the city:

> And the angel of the Lord went forth,
> and slew a hundred and eighty-five
> thousand in the camp of the Assyrians;
> and when men arose early in the morning,
> behold these were all dead bodies.
> Isaiah 37:36 (RSV)

Biblical commentators differ on the application of this verse, but there is in fact an intriguing extrabiblical account of an Assyrian army being decimated by mice on a campaign near the Egyptian border, where the rodents are said to have eaten the bowstrings and other equipment of the Assyrian army and perhaps to have triggered a deadly bout of a disease such as the bubonic plague.

In any case, as the king's advisors and Jerusalem's defenders stood on the city wall that day, facing a mighty, alien horde, the situation looked grim. The crafty Rabshakeh took full advantage.

> And the Rabshakeh said to them, "Say to Hezekiah,
> 'Thus says the great king, the king of Assyria:
> On what do you rest this confidence of yours?
> Do you think that mere words are strategy and power for war?
> On whom do you now rely, that you have rebelled against me?
> Behold, you are relying on Egypt, that broken reed of a staff,
> which will pierce the hand of any man who leans on it.
> Such is Pharaoh king of Egypt to all who rely on him.
> But if you say to me, "We rely on the Lord our God,"
> is it not he whose high
> places and altars Hezekiah has removed,
> saying to Judah and to Jerusalem,
> "You shall worship before this altar"?
> Come now, make a wager with my master the king of Assyria:
> I will give you two thousand horses,
> if you are able on your part to set riders upon them.
> How then can you repulse a single captain
> among the least of my master's servants,
> when you rely on Egypt for chariots and for horsemen . . .'"
> Isaiah 36:4–9 (RSV)

One after the other, the Rabshakeh dismantled the arguments undergirding Jerusalem's resistance. "Negotiations won't save you; mere words are useless now. Your allies, the Egyptians, are hopelessly unreliable." (Indeed, the Assyrians defeated an Egyptian army in an important battle during this very campaign.) Ironically, Isaiah and the Rabshakeh were on the same page as far as Egypt's unreliability was concerned! "Military resources? You don't have enough men or equipment to field a chariot battalion against us even if we gave you the horses." The Rabshakeh even tried to undermine Judah's religious resolve by referring to Hezekiah's recent reforms (the nature of which the Rabshakeh misunderstood). But the biggest blow of all came with the Rabshakeh's claim that, in fact, the Hebrew god was on the side of the Assyrians,

> "Moreover, is it without the Lord
> that I have come up against the land
> to destroy it? The LORD said to me,
> 'Go up against this land, and destroy it.'"
> Isaiah 36:10 (RSV)

Isaiah's own prophecies were now turned against him and his people. For, previously Isaiah had very publicly announced God's intentions:

> Ah, Assyria, the rod of my anger, the staff of my fury!
> Against a godless nation I send him,
> and against the people of my wrath
> I command him . . .
> Isaiah 10:5–6a (RSV)

and

> In that day the Lord will shave with a razor
> which is hired beyond the River—
> with the king of Assyria . . .
> Isaiah 7:20a (RSV)

The Rabshakeh was clearly a master of psychological warfare, well-informed by his staff, and powerfully intimidating. King Hezekiah's representatives were overwhelmed. In one of the great ironies of Isaiah's career, the king now sent the same chief of staff and secretary of state along with the "senior priests" of the land—deliberately clad in the garments of penitence and humiliation—to seek the help of the prophet, Isaiah, the very one whose message they had previously scorned.

> They said to him, "Thus says Hezekiah.
> 'This is a day of distress, of rebuke,
> and of disgrace; children have come to the birth,
> and there is no strength to bring them forth.

> It may be that the LORD your God heard the words of the Rabshakeh,
> whom his master the king of Assyria
> has sent to mock the living God,
> and will rebuke the words which the LORD your God has heard;
> therefore lift up your prayer for the remnant that is left.'"
> Isaiah 37:3–4 (RSV)

For Isaiah this was major vindication. But it was almost too late. "Children have come to the birth with no strength to bring them forth" was probably a popular way of saying, "It's hopeless; there is no future now." But what is even more striking here is that the temple priests are presented as referring to "your God" when addressing Isaiah: "It may be that *your* God heard the words of the Rabshakeh . . . and will rebuke the words which the Lord *your* God has heard" (Isaiah 36:4, italics added), as if Isaiah had a divine connection which they, the leading religious leaders, did not. Whether intended or not, these words aptly depict the estrangement of God's people which Isaiah's prophecies had addressed all along and which had led to their finding themselves in this situation in the first place. The people of Jerusalem were indeed a remnant now; they were all that was left intact of two proud nations of God's people. Eventually even they would be reduced to an even smaller community, let into exile in Babylon and finally dispersed throughout the centuries to follow.

Isaiah rose to the occasion. Reciting two of the great phrases of prophetic proclamation, Isaiah responded, "Thus says the Lord: Do not be afraid . . ." (Isaiah 36:6). God, Isaiah announces, "will put a spirit in him [the king of Assyria], so that he shall hear a rumor, and return to his own land; and I will make him fall by the sword in his own land" (Isaiah 37:7, RSV). Later in the text Isaiah is quoted as declaring,

> "Therefore thus says the Lord concerning the king of Assyria:
> He shall not come into this city, or shoot an arrow there,
> or come before it with a shield, or cast up a siege mound against it.
> By the way that he came, by the same he shall return,
> and he shall not come into this city, says the LORD."
> Isaiah 37:33–34 (RSV)

Isaiah proved right. Jerusalem did not fall. The king of Assyria withdrew. Twenty years later Sennacherib was indeed stabbed to death by his own sons, as Assyrian court records confirm. The fact that the writer of this section of the book of Isaiah (recording these events) probably knew about that reminds us that this historical account was composed, at least in part, many years later.

It also reminds us to look for more than just history here. For, a more important message is contained in these texts. We see it especially in Hezekiah's response to the letter he received from the king of Assyria after the Rabshakeh subsequently left Jerusalem to rejoin the Assyrian king in order to help him confront a changing military situation. The Assyrian king's letter said,

> "Thus shall you speak to Hezekiah king of Judah:
> 'Do not let your God on whom you rely deceive you
> by promising that Jerusalem
> will not be given into the hand of the king of Assyria.
> Behold, you have heard what the kings of Assyria have done
> to all lands, destroying them utterly.
> And shall you be delivered?
> Have the gods of the nations delivered them,
> the nations which my fathers destroyed . . . ?'"
> Isaiah 37:10–12 (RSV)

Sennacherib's letter went on to actually name the nations and kings whose gods had failed them. Hezekiah understood exactly what was at stake. So he did what most of us would do in a similar situation. He played the religious card.

> Hezekiah received the letter from the hand of the messengers,
> and read it; and Hezekiah went up to the house of the Lord,
> and spread it before the Lord.
> And Hezekiah prayed to the Lord, "O Lord of hosts, God of Israel,
> who art enthroned above the cherubim, thou art the God,
> thou alone, of all the kingdoms of the earth;
> thou hast made heaven and earth.
> Incline thy ear, O Lord, and hear; open thy eyes,
> O Lord, and see; and hear all the words of Sennacherib,
> which he has sent to mock the living God.
> Of a truth, O Lord, the kings of Assyria have laid waste
> all the nations and their lands, and have cast their gods
> into the fire; for they were no gods,
> but the worship of men's hands, wood and stone;
> therefore they were destroyed.
> So now, O Lord, our God, save us from his hand,
> that all the kingdoms of the earth may know
> that thou alone art the Lord."
> Isaiah 37:14–20 (RSV)

Long a faithful man who had sought to reform and revive his people's faith—despite political winds to the contrary—Hezekiah had now, in the crucial moment, returned to the core commitment of his life. All that had passed, politically, religiously, militarily, and otherwise, came down to one fundamental realization: God was ultimately in charge of the situation. On behalf of the nation, Hezekiah, the humbled king, makes the critical confession, "thou alone art the God, thou alone, of all the kingdoms of the earth."

At this point Isaiah reemerges to deliver God's response to Hezekiah's recognition.

> Then Isaiah the son of Amoz sent to Hezekiah, saying,
> "Thus says the Lord, the God of Israel:
> Because you have prayed to me concerning Sennacherib
> king of Assyria, this is the word that the LORD
> has spoken concerning him . . .
> 'By your servants you have mocked the LORD . . .
> Have you not heard that I determined it long ago?
> I planned from days of old what now I bring to pass . . .
> 'I know your sitting down and your going out and coming in,
> and your raging against me . . .
> I will put my hook in your nose and my bit in your mouth,
> and I will turn you back on the way by which you came!'"
> Isaiah 37:21, 24a, 26, 28, 29b (RSV)

The battle between Assyria and Judah is now a personal battle between human hubris and the living God, the God who knows everything, even the "sitting down" and "going out and coming in" of the king of Assyria. The whole historical encounter is thus transformed into a testimony of faith.

> "It may be that the Lord your God heard the words of the Rabshakeh,
> whom his master the king of Assyria
> has sent to mock the living God,
> and will rebuke the words which the LORD your God has heard."
> Isaiah 37:4 (RSV)

So spoke the sackcloth priests to Isaiah, hoping to save their skins. "So now, O LORD, our God, save us from his hand, that all the kingdoms of the earth may know that thou alone art the Lord," prayed Hezekiah. It was almost as though the speakers were appealing to God's ego or pointing out the publicity value to their God of divine intervention. But from

God confronting Pharaoh with the ten plagues in Egypt to the confrontation between Elijah and the prophets of Baal on Mt. Carmel, history had shown that God had repeatedly defended God's people in the crisis moments that defined their destiny.

In such a moment it was fitting that God's prophet has the determinative say. Isaiah's closing prophecy (perhaps one of his last) is a reiteration of the sovereignty of God over all history and people, calling his listeners back to faith.

> "And this shall be the sign for you:
> this year eat what grows of itself,
> and in the second year what springs of the same;
> then in the third year sow and
> reap, and plant vineyards, and eat their fruit.
> And the surviving remnant of the
> house of Judah shall again take root downward,
> and bear fruit upward;
> for out of Jerusalem shall go forth a remnant,
> and out of Mount Zion a band of survivors.
> The zeal of the LORD of hosts will accomplish this."
> Isaiah 37:30–32 (RSV)

The armies of Sennacherib had no doubt ravaged the countryside, scavenging grain, raiding food supplies, and disrupting the normal cycles of an agricultural economy. But over time, Isaiah reassured people, things would return to normal and the Assyrians would be gone. Even if there were destroyers in the future, such as the Babylonians proved to be, a remnant would survive. This was God's sure promise. "For I will defend this city to save it, for my own sake and for the sake of my servant David" (Isaiah 37:35). Some among Isaiah's people interpreted this declaration as a pledge to preserve Jerusalem itself as inviolable forever. But Jerusalem's fall to the Babylonians one hundred years later disproved that assumption and demonstrated that God's plan is for a people not for mere nations or human constructs.

When it was all over, the people of Jerusalem had survived. The siege was lifted. A semblance of normality returned. The Rabshakeh, as far as we know, was never heard from again. Things turned out as Hezekiah, the priests, and Isaiah had hoped. God would not be mocked.

For Discussion

1. Sometimes Scripture offers multiple versions of the same story. There are two creation accounts (Genesis 1 and 2), three stories about who Abraham and Isaac said their wives were (Genesis 12:10–20, 20:2, and 26:6–11), and variations between the books of Kings and Chronicles regarding the history of the nations of Israel and Judah. Rarely however, do three different books use almost exactly the same words to describe a particular event as do Isaiah 36–37, 2 Kings 18, and 2 Chronicles 32. Even more interesting than the similarities are the differences: the Isaiah version focuses on a theological point; 2 Kings is more historical in nature; 2 Chronicles, in turn, comes across as a happy summary designed to make its leading figures look good.

   The Isaiah account omits a hugely critical piece of information found in 2 Kings, namely, three verses (2 Kings 18:14–16) which record that Hezekiah actually surrendered to Sennacherib, apologized for rebelling, and paid an enormous ransom to save his city. That key tidbit raises all kinds of questions. If Hezekiah had already surrendered, for example, why was the Rabshakeh threatening Jerusalem? Had Sennacherib changed his mind, regretting his leniency and subsequently demanding unconditional surrender? Had Egypt already been defeated by Assyria, thus motivating Hezekiah's surrender? If so, why did the Rabshakeh refer to them as still an active ally of Judah? If Hezekiah had already paid a ransom, why was the Rabshakeh threatening deportation (a process that went on for over forty years with the defeated tribes of the northern kingdom)? Why does the text say that Sennacherib went to fight king Tirhakah when Egyptian records show that at the time Tirhakah was probably only about ten years old and not yet king? Do the Isaiah and 2 Kings accounts blend together records from two separate attacks by Sennacherib perhaps a decade or more apart?

   What does it matter? Is it fair to measure biblical records such as these—which are unquestionably grounded in actual history—by modern academic standards (which are sometimes pretty subjective themselves)? What is most important for you about Scripture—its historicity, its spiritual impact, its stories about people like us and how they experienced God in their lives, or what?

2. The armies of powers both great and small have been marching back and forth across the Middle East for all of recorded history, destroying cities, devastating populations, repeatedly drenching the region in blood and suffering. Do you think it will ever end?

For Reflection

> Hezekiah received the letter from the hand of the messengers and read it; and Hezekiah went up to the house of the Lord, and spread it before the Lord. And Hezekiah prayed . . ."
> Isaiah 37:14–15 (RSV)

Have you ever spread a letter before the Lord, a letter that describes your life, the choices you have made, the crises you have faced, the threats you have encountered? Write your own letter; record the questions you have, the fears and doubts that still unsettle you. Be as specific as Hezekiah was, naming his adversary. Then list the factors that give you the confidence and hope to bring this letter before God and dare to lay it open. About what are you sure? How would you like God to respond? You could write that down, too. Are you able to confess as Hezekiah did, "Thou art the God, thou alone, of all the kingdoms of the earth"?

For Prayer

As Hezekiah prayed, "Incline thy ear, O Lord, and hear; open thy eyes, O Lord, and see," so do we also pray, O Lord, for your attentive presence in our lives. Give us courage in the face of danger and distress and the reassurance that you will sustain and deliver us through all adversity into an abundant new life. Amen.

35

Hjelmer and the Babylonians

"Remember now, O Lord . . .
Lo, it was for my welfare that I had great bitterness . . .
The LORD will save me,
and we will sing to stringed instruments
all the days of our life at the house of the LORD."

ISAIAH 38:3A, 17A, 20 (RSV)

HJELMER LAY STILL AND cold on the hospital gurney, barrel-chested, his thick-muscled arms and big hands limp at his side. The red LED on the blood pressure monitor receiving signals from his fingertip registered 34, a number normally indicative that a person was all but dead.

Then Hjelmer stirred. The old Norwegian bachelor farmer—whose strong genes, hard labor, and diet of red meat, potatoes, butter, sugared coffee with sweets, and an occasional shot of liquor had kept him healthy and as strong as an ox for over eight decades—twitched. His eyes opened enough to let him take in the sterile room and his pastor standing beside him. "So," he intoned in a low but steady voice with his classic Minnesota immigrant-heritage accent, "who do ya' tink vil vin da gov'ner's race dis year?" A few weeks later, back on the farm and recovered from his ordeal, Hjelmer was able to discover the answer for himself.

> In those days Hezekiah became sick and was at the point of death.
> And Isaiah the prophet the son of Amoz came to him,
> and said to him,
> "Thus says the LORD: Set your house in order; for you shall die,
> you shall not recover." Then Hezekiah turned his face to the wall,
> and prayed to the LORD, and said,

"Remember now, O Lord, I beseech thee,
how I have walked before thee in faithfulness
and with a whole heart,
and have done what is good in thy sight."
And Hezekiah wept bitterly.
Isaiah 38:1–3 (RSV)

Who would not have wept in Hezekiah's place? His city was under siege by an Assyrian army. The kingdom he had rebuilt was once again shattered. His people faced potential defeat and slavery. Understandably, the accumulated stress and trauma came pouring out at what now seemed like the end of all that he had worked for and loved.

In the noontide of my days I must depart;
I am consigned to the gates of Sheol for the rest of my years.
I said, I shall not see the Lord in the land of the living;
I shall look upon mortals no more . . .
My dwelling is plucked up and removed from me
like a shepherd's tent;
like a weaver I have rolled up my life; he cuts me off from the loom . . .
Isaiah 38:10–12 (NRSV)

Remarkably, Hezekiah did not beg. He did not plead for his people or his city when he first heard Isaiah's pronouncement. Rather, he accepted his fate, asking God simply to remember that he had done his best to be faithful.

Later, in a psalm that was composed for formal recitation in the temple, "after he had been sick and recovered" (Isaiah 38:9), Hezekiah's testimony included the kind of pleas which we all utter at some point in life: "Oh, restore me to health and make me live!" (Isaiah 39:16b).

God responded. In fact, God had a change of heart that surprised even Isaiah, proving that even a prophet's proclamations are not irreversible when circumstances change.

Then the word of the Lord came to Isaiah:
"Go and say to Hezekiah,
Thus says the Lord, the God of David your father:
I have heard your prayer, I have seen your tears;
behold, I will add fifteen years to your life.
I will deliver you and this city out of the hand of the king of Assyria,
and defend this city."
Isaiah 38: 4–6 (RSV)

In 2 Kings 20, there is an almost identical version of this story. It is interesting to note that there (as we might put it today) Isaiah doesn't even make it back to his car in the parking lot before he has to turn around and correct his previous pronouncement.

> And before Isaiah had gone out of the middle court,
> the word of the LORD came to him:
> "Turn back, and say to Hezekiah the prince of my people . . .
> I will heal you . . ."
> 2 Kings 20:4 (RSV)

One wonders how Isaiah felt about that. Did he feel foolish or just take it in stride as all in a prophet's day's work?

Both texts—2 Kings and Isaiah 38—are intended to do more than just tell a good story, of course. When Isaiah's second message says, "Thus says the LORD, the God of David your father" for instance, a whole other layer of meaning is exposed. David, after all, was not literally Hezekiah's father. Rather, Hezekiah was a king in an ancestral line traceable back to David. God had created and preserved this royal line for centuries already and was now preserving Hezekiah as part of that covenant. Jerusalem was David's city and God was about to preserve Jerusalem as well.

It was no accident that Isaiah's second message connects Hezekiah's recovery with God's protection of Jerusalem. "And I will add fifteen years to your life. I will deliver you *and* this city for your sake and for my servant David's sake" (2 Kings 20:6, RSV, italics added). Hezekiah's sickness and Jerusalem's siege were parallel events. As Hezekiah's model piety contributed to his recovery, so did the pious submission of the king contribute to the sparing of Jerusalem, at least from the perspective of the recorder of these events. But neither Jerusalem nor the Davidic line were guaranteed protection forever. As the keepers of Hebrew history attributed the demise of the northern kingdom to unfaithful behavior, so later did they explain the eventual fall of Jerusalem and the collapse of the Davidic line in a similar way. Hezekiah's story thus became more than an account of events in his own time. It served as an explanation for events that occurred many years later in the face of further adversity. We find that kind of deeper meaning in Hezekiah's psalm.

> Surely, it was for my welfare that I had great bitterness;
> but you have held back my life from the pit of destruction,
> for you have cast all my sin behind your back.
> For Sheol cannot thank you, death cannot praise you;

> those who go down to the Pit cannot hope for your faithfulness.
> The living, the living, they thank you, as I do this day;
> fathers make known to the children your faithfulness.
> Isaiah 38:17–19 (NRSV)

Hezekiah became a witness to God's greater purpose. His experience testified not simply to a personal deliverance and to a city's survival, but to the One who is the ultimate Author of all life's events. "But what can I say? For he has spoken to me, and he himself has done it" (Isaiah 38:15a, RSV). Recognizing that God's hand was at work provided testimony to generations to come of the living God who seeks human welfare, who can "cast all [one's] sins behind your back." In Hezekiah's case, with the Assyrians perched at the city gates challenging the power of the Hebrews' God, Hezekiah's recovery and Jerusalem's deliverance constituted a testimony that endures to this day. Still, Hezekiah asked Isaiah for a sign to reassure him.

> And Hezekiah said to Isaiah,
> "What shall be the sign that the Lord will heal me,
> and that I shall go up to the house of the LORD
> on the third day?" . . .
> And Isaiah the prophet cried to the LORD;
> and he brought the shadow back ten steps,
> by which the sun had declined on the dial of Ahaz.
> 2 Kings 20:8, 11 (RSV)

Here again, we find layers of meaning, a story within a story. When Joshua and the Israelites had faced a great army centuries earlier, God was said to have miraculously intervened, "stopping the sun" until victory was won (Joshua 10:12-13). Hezekiah would have known that story since childhood. "The shadow . . . by which the sun had declined on the dial of Ahaz" could also be understood as referring to Ahaz himself, Hezekiah's predecessor, whose faithless deeds had helped usher in the darkness Hezekiah now faced and which God was promising to reverse. In feckless fear King Ahaz had declined God's offer of a sign from Isaiah, thereby incurring God's wrath (Isaiah 7:10–17). In contrast, Hezekiah—the faithful king—could freely ask for God's assurance directly. The sign itself was less important than the meanings it carried and the hope it gave to Hezekiah for the trial he faced.

As we know, Hezekiah recovered and Jerusalem survived. But those events in turn signaled the inauguration of a new chapter in the history of God's people. For now a new character entered the story.

> At that time Merodach-baladan the son of Baladan, king of Babylon,
> sent envoys with letters and a present to Hezekiah,
> for he had heard that he had been sick and had recovered.
> Isaiah 39:1–2 (RSV)

Hezekiah's illness is presented as the link to a terrible new future. For, Babylon rises to become the power that defeats the Assyrians. But in a macabre twist of fate, the Babylonian leader who ostensibly reaches out in friendship, bearing gifts to Hezekiah, presages the arrival of a Babylonian army just over a century later that will decimate Jerusalem, burn Solomon's temple to the ground, and obliterate the royal heritage to which Hezekiah belongs.

The prophet Isaiah suspected as much. Already a well-known critic of imprudent alliances, Isaiah here represents the voice of caution, warning of disaster ahead. He asks three questions. Where do these people come from? What did they say? What have they seen?

Merodach-baladan was a real king, a contemporary of Hezekiah's, whose resistance to the Assyrians is historically documented. That his envoys met with Hezekiah and his court to plot rebellion against the Assyrians in the company of such parties as the Egyptians or the people of Ashdod is thoroughly believable.

The concern expressed by Isaiah, however, was what risks such alliances could entail. Were the Babylonian envoys also spies, scoping out Hezekiah's weaknesses and assets? What was their true intent?

> Then Isaiah said to Hezekiah, "Hear the word of the Lord of hosts:
> Behold, the days are coming, when all that is in your house,
> and that which your fathers have stored up till this day,
> shall be carried to Babylon; nothing shall be left, says, the LORD.
> And some of your own sons, who are born to you,
> shall be taken away;
> and they shall be eunuchs in the palace of the king of Babylon."
> Isaiah 39:5–7 (RSV)

The whole of the book of Isaiah to this point—thirty-nine chapters—has been set against the background of the Assyrian conquest of the northern kingdom of Israel and eventually the bulk of Judah as well. Now suddenly the topic shifts to Babylon. However, there are no detailed stories of conquest and siege, no accounts of the kind of personal encounters and prophetic intervention that we have see with Isaiah, Ahaz, and Hezekiah.

Rather, chapter 40 of the book of Isaiah begins with the announcement of the end of the Babylonian Exile, a hundred and fifty years later.

> Comfort, comfort my people, says your God.
> Speak tenderly to Jerusalem
> and cry to her that her warfare has ended,
> that her iniquity is pardoned . . .
> Isaiah 40:1–2a (RSV)

Like the end of a movie setting up its sequel, chapter 39 introduces the new villain and ends with an ominous warning of conflicts to come. It serves as the bridge between two great sections in the book of Isaiah and two great chapters in the history of God's people.

In response to Isaiah's dire declaration about Babylon, Hezekiah makes an unusual reply.

> Then said Hezekiah to Isaiah,
> "The word of the LORD which you have spoken is good."
> For he thought, "There will be peace and security in my days."
> Isaiah 39:8 (RSV)

Okay, so Hezekiah had just had a personal death sentence lifted, and was understandably relieved. But was he really being callous and self-focused, as if to say, "I got mine, so I don't really care what happens to others?" That's not likely from the king who had devoted his life to his people. More likely, this is the author's way of trying to conclude a story of deliverance with a note of relief, symbolized by Hezekiah's ability to live out his life with his nation secure and at peace, albeit as a vassal state. Yet it may also reflect the hard reality faced by regents both before Hezekiah and ever since, namely, that there is only so much a king or a queen or a president can do. The rest is up to history . . . and, if you believe as Hezekiah and Isaiah did, God.

For Discussion

1. Hezekiah asked, "What shall be the sign that the LORD will heal me?" (2 Kings 20:8, RSV). Hezekiah seems to just assume that evidence of God's promised healing will be forthcoming. What do you assume or expect of God? What kind of signs would satisfy your need for

assurance of God's active presence?

2. "I shall go up to the house of the LORD on the third day" (2 Kings 20:8). There is an intentional connection between Hezekiah's healing and a religious recognition of it. "I shall not see the LORD in the land of the living," (Isaiah 38:11a) Hezekiah had lamented. "Seeing the LORD" was another way to describe worshiping with one's community in the majestic Jerusalem temple. How important to you is connecting the key events of your life—healings, celebrations, moments of relief or joy—to worship and community?

For Reflection

Isaiah warned, "Set your house in order; for you shall die" (Isaiah 38:1). He could say the same thing to any of us today. Yet wills, trusts, and estate planning are anxious activities for most of us. It's hard to let go, to truly face what Hezekiah did: "like a weaver I have rolled up my life; he cuts me off from the loom" (Isaiah 38:12, RSV). What do you need to do to "set your house in order"—financially, relationally, spiritually—before your life is "rolled up?"

Look at death. Like Hamlet holding Yorrick's skull, examine your end. Can you imagine a peaceful reintegration with the earth from which you came? Can you envision your place among the ancestors, the amorphous cloud which creates the heritage of descendents as yet unborn? What immediate memories do you wish that those who know you will keep alive for another generation? Who is the genuine "you" that you want others to hold onto? Which "you" will God remember?

For Prayer

Remember us, now, O LORD, as you remembered your servant Hezekiah and as you have remembered countless others who have turned their faces to you. Hear our prayers and see our tears as you have heard and seen and responded to the cries and supplications of your people for centuries. Help us to make your faithfulness known to our children and to all who come after, with a song of thanksgiving that will last all the days of our lives. Amen.

36

Polar Opposites

"He will be the stability of your times . . ."

ISAIAH 33:6A (RSV)

IS THE UNIVERSE SUSPENDED between polar opposites: matter and anti-matter, darkness and light, life and death? Most television shows and movies are clearly premised on themes such as good and evil, hero and villain, "the Force" and its dark side. Scripture itself begins with the confrontation between chaos and order and ends with destruction and new creation. We live between God and no-God, birth and non-existence, ignorance and knowledge. Even the proverbial shades of gray depend on there being the polar opposites of white and black.

The book of Isaiah captures this kind of dichotomy in life, perhaps nowhere moreso than in two of the chapters that may once have served as the summarizing conclusion to Isaiah's prophetic testimony. Chapters 34 and 35 have been described as an *Inferno and Paradiso*, a presentation of polar opposites describing life in conflict with God's will and life blessed by God's grace, or, put another way, heaven and hell spelled out in earthly terms.

> Draw near, O nations, to hear, and hearken, O peoples!
> Let the earth listen, and all that fills it; the world,
> and all that comes from it.
> For the LORD is enraged against all the nations,
> and furious against all their host,
> he has doomed them, has given them over for slaughter.
> Isaiah 34:1–2 (RSV)

The prophetic claim was consistently universal. Isaiah's God was never just the God of Israel. The God of whom Isaiah spoke was sovereign over all nations, all times, all peoples, everything. Accordingly, God's wrath was universal. One of the polar extremes describing what that could mean was spelled out clearly by Isaiah and other prophets.

> Behold, the day of the Lord comes, cruel,
> with wrath and fierce anger,
> to make the earth a desolation and to destroy its sinners from it . . .
> I will punish the world for its evil, and the wicked for their iniquity;
> I will put an end to the pride of the arrogant,
> and lay low the haughtiness of the ruthless.
> Isaiah 13:9, 11 (RSV)

In multiple places the book of Isaiah depicts the futility of human hubris, the end of alternatives for all life, the destruction beyond which there is no redemption or recovery possible. Creation itself is marked as destructible: "All the host of heaven shall rot away, the skies roll up like a scroll" (Isaiah 34:4a, RSV).

> Therefore I will make the heavens tremble,
> and the earth will be shaken out of its place,
> at the wrath of the LORD of hosts in the day of his fierce anger.
> Isaiah 13:13 (RSV)

To convey God's total sovereignty, God's absolute power, the reality beyond which nothing further could be imagined, it was necessary to illustrate that totality in vivid terms. Unfortunately, for the people of a land called Edom—a neighboring tribe of Judah which actually shared a common ancestry—this meant not only their utter annihilation but also their becoming the "poster tribe," or historical prototype, for divine retribution.

> For my sword has drunk its fill in the heavens;
> behold, it descends for judgment on Edom,
> upon the people I have doomed . . .
> For the LORD has a day of vengeance,
> a year of recompense for the cause of Zion.
> And the streams of Edom shall be turned to pitch
> and her soil into brimstone;
> her land shall become burning pitch.
> Night and day it shall not be quenched;
> its smoke shall go up for ever.

From generation to generation it shall lie waste,
none shall pass through it for ever and ever.
Isaiah 34:5, 8–10 (RSV)

Scholars have pondered why Edom was singled out for such condemnation. Though a thorn in Judah's side as far back as David's day, Edom's offenses were hardly worse than those of other adversaries, although after the Babylonian Exile, Edom repeatedly sought to undermine Judah's recovery. Internecine conflict is often the most bitter.

Edom, however, is not entirely alone in serving as an example of the extreme desolation that God's punishment can produce. The Babylonians, too—an unrelated people—were also singled out to exemplify the totality of God's eradicating wrath.

And Babylon, the glory of kingdoms,
the splendor and pride of the Chaldeans,
will be like Sodom and Gomorrah when God overthrew them.
It will never be inhabited or dwelt in for all generations . . .
But wild beasts will lie down there,
and its house will be full of howling creatures;
there ostriches will dwell, and there satyrs will dance.
Hyenas will cry in its towers, and jackals in the pleasant palaces.
Isaiah 13:19–22a (RSV)

In First Isaiah there are two frequent symbols of permanent obliteration. The first—referred to three times (Isaiah 1:10; 13:19; and 34:9–10)—was the fiery destruction visited upon Sodom and Gomorrah in Abraham's day, an event which became a biblical archetype that continues to this day. The second symbol of permanent obliteration came from nature—the image of beasts, wild animals and strange creatures taking up residence in the ruins of decimated cities. For Babylon it was hyenas and "howling creatures." For Edom it was everything from hawks and porcupines to "the night hag," a reference to a destructive witchlike creature from Babylonian mythology.

But the hawk and the porcupine shall possess it,
the owl and the raven shall dwell in it . . .
Thorns shall grow over its strongholds,
nettles and thistles in its fortresses.
It shall be the haunt of jackals, an abode for ostriches.
And wild beasts shall meet with hyenas,
the satyr shall cry to his fellow;

> yea, there shall the night hag alight,
> and find for herself a resting place.
> Isaiah 34:11a, 13–14 (RSV)

In other words, order gives way to chaos where God is absent. Life becomes wild, frightening, and dangerous. The return of chaos to Edom is referred to explicitly in the Hebrew with the same words used in Genesis 1:2 to describe the world before God's creative activity, when the world was "without form and void" (*tohu* and *bohu*). "He shall stretch the line of confusion (*bohu*) over it, and the plummet of chaos (*tohu*) over its nobles" (Isaiah 34:11, RSV). Edom will even lose its name, its identity as a livable place, "They shall name it No Kingdom There, and all its princes shall be nothing" (Isaiah 34:12, RSV).

With all these images of abandonment and destruction Isaiah paints a picture of what life lived at odds with God's will produces. To be sure, such words of judgment resonated with an oppressed people. The suffering endured by Isaiah's people over centuries of conflict—whether from the Assyrians or Babylonians—surely fed a thirst for revenge. But beyond vengeance, the greater point was always that life without God was untenable if not unthinkable altogether.

This was the polar opposite at one end of the spectrum. At the other end were the incredible possibilities of life lived in harmony with God, also spelled out repeatedly in the grand vision which Isaiah cultivated not just for his own people but for all who came after them. Isaiah prophesied that a day will come when

> The Spirit is poured upon us from on high,
> and the wilderness becomes a fruitful field . . .
> Then justice will dwell in the wilderness,
> and righteousness abide in the fruitful field.
> And the effect of righteousness will be peace,
> and the result of righteousness,
> quietness and trust for ever.
> My people will abide in a peaceful habitation,
> in secure dwellings, and in quiet resting places . . .
> Isaiah 32:15–18 (RSV)

Whereas one of the symbols of chaos was nature out of balance—storms, drought, wild beasts, the heavens themselves in peril—a mark of the alternative is nature overflowing with abundance:

The wilderness and the dry land shall be glad,
the desert shall rejoice and blossom . . .
then shall the lame man leap like a hart,
and the tongue of the dumb sing for joy.
For waters shall break forth in the wilderness
and streams in the desert;
the burning sand shall become a pool,
and the thirsty ground springs of water;
the haunt of jackals shall become a swamp,
the grass shall become reeds and rushes.
Isaiah 35:1, 6–7 (RSV)

Nature is even personified as having its own voice for joining a chorus of celebration: "like the crocus, it shall blossom abundantly, and rejoice with joy and singing" (Isaiah 35:1–2a, RSV). "Carmel and Sharon," geographical areas of prosperity and beauty in Israel, served as symbols of desolation in the dark times:

The land mourns and languishes;
Lebanon is confounded and withers away;
Sharon is like a desert;
and Bashan and Carmel shake off their leaves.
Isaiah 33:9 (RSV)

But in the vision of the positive polar opposite, their fertility is restored:

The glory of Lebanon shall be given to it,
the majesty of Carmel and Sharon.
They shall see the glory of the Lord,
the majesty of our God.
Isaiah 35:2b (RSV)

Human society itself will become a place of order, common sense, and fairness, according to the vision cultivated by Isaiah and his followers:

See, a king will reign in righteousness
and princes will rule in justice . . .
The minds of the rash will have good judgment . . .
A fool will no more be called noble,
nor a villain said to be honorable.
For fools speak folly and their minds plot iniquity:
to practice ungodliness,
to utter error concerning the Lord,

to leave the craving of the hungry unsatisfied,
and to deprive the thirsty of drink.
Isaiah 32:1, 4a, 5, 6 (NRSV)

On that day . . . The meek shall obtain fresh joy in the Lord,
and the neediest people shall exult in the Holy One of Israel.
For the tyrant shall be no more, and the scoffer shall cease to be;
all those alert to do evil shall be cut off—
those who cause a person to lose a lawsuit . . .
and without grounds deny justice to the one in the right.
Isaiah 29:18–21 (NRSV)

The character of those who live in the positive polar reality envisioned by Isaiah will be like those deemed worthy to enter God's presence in the temple at Jerusalem:

"Who among us can live with the devouring fire?
Who among us can live with everlasting flames?"
Those who walk righteously and speak uprightly,
who despise the gain of oppression,
who wave away a bribe instead of accepting it,
who stop their ears from hearing of bloodshed
and shut their eyes from looking on evil . . ."
Isaiah 33:14b–16 (NRSV)

In the positive polar reality to which God seeks to draw us, burdens will be lifted and beauty will take their place:

Your eyes will see the king in his beauty;
they will behold a land that stretches afar.
Your mind will muse on the terror:
"Where is he who counted,
where is he who weighed the tribute?
Where is he who counted the towers?"
You will see no more the insolent people.
The people of an obscure speech
which you cannot comprehend,
stammering in a tongue which you cannot understand.
Isaiah 33:17–19 (RSV)

Whether "the terror" is Assyrian, Babylonian, or of twenty-first century making, it will become a thing of the past. Instead of terror, there will be healing, available to all: "And no inhabitant will say, 'I am sick . . .'" (Isaiah 33:24a, RSV). "In that day the deaf shall hear . . . the eyes of the blind shall see" (Isaiah 29:18, RSV).

When Isaiah had his famous vision in the temple, inaugurating his prophetic career, he was told to

> "'Make the heart of this people fat, and their ears heavy,
> and shut their eyes, lest they see with their eyes,
> and hear with their ears,
> and understand with their hearts,
> and turn and be healed.'"
> Isaiah 6:10 (RSV)

Decades later, his mission was reversed and he was able to lift up before his people the vision of an alternative.

> Then the eyes of the blind shall be opened,
> and the ears of the deaf unstopped;
> then the lame shall leap like a deer,
> and the tongue of the speechless sing for joy.
> Isaiah 35:5–6 (NRSV)

There is a way forward, a path beyond ignorance, fear, suffering, and injustice.

> And a highway shall be there and it shall be called the Holy Way;
> the unclean shall not travel on it, but it shall be for God's people,
> no traveler, not even fools, shall go astray.
> No lion [danger] shall be there,
> nor shall any ravenous beast come up on it;
> they shall not be found there, but the redeemed shall walk there.
> Isaiah 35:8–10 (NRSV)

A hundred years after Isaiah, words like these must have given great hope and encouragement to Isaiah's people as their time of exile in Babylon neared an end. Chapters 40–55 of the book of Isaiah, addressing that period, resonate with similar images of redemption. But the vision first articulated by Isaiah transcended both his own time and the events that followed. It became a vision embedded in the hearts of people to this day.

The vision of a world without conflict or danger, where people live in prosperity and peace in a society where justice is realized—who dares dream that such a reality is indeed possible? Isaiah did. In a universe suspended between chaos and creation Isaiah described the worst that can happen and then pointed us to its polar opposite. He epitomized the breathtaking capacity of human beings to envision a new state of existence where nature itself is transformed, where humanity becomes whole, and where we live in the presence of a power that can save us. Isaiah's whole ministry witnessed to this power.

> Strengthen the weak hands, and make firm the feeble knees.
> Say to those who are of a fearful heart, "Be strong, fear not!
> Behold, your God will come . . . and save you."
> Isaiah 35:3–4 (RSV)

> The Lord is exulted . . . and he will be the stability of your times,
> abundance of salvation, wisdom, and knowledge . . .
> Isaiah 33:5a, 6a (RSV)

Isaiah's original calling came with a vision. His legacy is the vision he passed on to us. As inheritors of that vision we receive both comfort and responsibility. Who among us would not want such a vision to be realized, so that all people may live in the rich reality it depicts?

For Discussion

> And the ransomed of the Lord shall return,
> and come to Zion with singing;
> everlasting joy shall be upon their heads;
> they shall obtain joy and gladness,
> and sorrow and sighing shall flee away.
> Isaiah 35:10 (RSV)

1. Zion is much more than a city. It is also a dream, a symbol, an expression of where we experience and express joy and the release of all sorrow. What and where is Zion for you? Do you sense any portion of its presence around you in the physical world, in relationships, in worship? In a continuously changing, transient world where do you find what is immovable, permanent, sacred?
2. Do you agree with Isaiah? Does his model of "polar opposites" work for you, the dichotomy of near-apocalyptic threats on the one hand and fantastic promises on the other? Or would you prefer another approach?

For Reflection

Write a letter to Isaiah. Tell him what you think of his work and what you have learned from his life and his message. Imagine a dinner conversation with Isaiah. Would he be intimidating? Frightening? Entertaining? (Consider his propensity towards colorful language and his first-hand stories of dramatic political events and profound religious experiences).

Organize an Isaiah party. Role play some of the characters in his story. Recalling his many vineyard references, be sure to serve wine. Then raise a glass to Isaiah and toast this man who lived through such traumatic times, who talked directly to God, who endured rejection by his peers, and yet who left us with such extraordinary visions to feed our souls. Then ponder: what would he say to us now?

For Prayer

Sovereign God, thank you for Isaiah. Thank you for all those who give us visions of life as it *can* be—just, peaceful, blessed. Thank you for the love that speaks to us through prophet, text, and neighbor. Thank you for the triumph of Creation over chaos, light over darkness, life over death. Thank you for that awaiting day when all "sorrow and sighing shall flee away," when death will be swallowed up forever and all tears will be wiped away, when we "shall obtain joy and gladness" and when "the earth itself shall be full of the knowledge of the LORD," revealed both in nature and in human hearts. For that day we pray. Amen.

Bibliography

General Reference List

Black, Matthew, and H. H. Rowley. *Peake's Commentary on the Bible*. New York: Thomas Nelson, 1962.

Clements, Ronald E. *Isaiah 1–39*. New Century Bible Commentary. Grand Rapids: Eerdmans, 1980.

Collins, John Joseph. *Isaiah*. Collegeville, MN: The Liturgical Press, 1986.

Douglas, J. D., et al. *New Bible Dictionary*. 2nd ed. New York: Tyndale, 1982.

Drummond, Richard H. *Gautama the Buddha*. Grand Rapids: Eerdmans, 1974.

Harris, R. Laird, et al. *Theological Wordbook of the Old Testament*. Vols. 1–2. Chicago: Moody, 1980.

Lull, Timothy F. *On Being Lutheran*. Minneapolis: Augsburg Fortress, 2006.

Lutheran Book of Worship. Minneapolis: Augsburg, 1978.

Metzger, Bruce M., and Michael D. Coogan. *Oxford Companion to the Bible*. New York: Oxford University Press, 1993.

Neill, Stephen. *A History of Christian Missions*. Harmondsworth: Penguin, 1964.

Packer, J. I., et al. *The Bible Almanac*. Nashville: Thomas Nelson, 1980.

Smith, Huston. *The Religions of Man*. New York: Harper and Row, 1958.

von Rad, Gerhard. *Old Testament Theology*. Vol 2. Translated by D. M. G. Stalker. New York: Harper & Row, 1965.

Reference Bibles

Lutheran Study Bible. NRSV. Minneapolis: Augsburg Fortress, 2009.

New Oxford Annotated Bible with the Apocrypha. RSV. New York: Oxford University Press, 1977.

NIV *Interlinear Hebrew-English Old Testament*. Grand Rapids, MI: Regency Reference Library, 1987.

Serendipity Student Bible. NIV. Littleton, CO: Serendipity House and Grand Rapids, MI: Zondervan, 1997.

Selected Internet Resources

Chapter 5: The Heavens

"Enuma Elish, The Epic of Creation." In *The Seven Tablets of Creation*. Translated by L. W. King. London, 1902. Online: http://www.sacred-texts.com/ane/enuma.htm.

"Tiamat." *Encyclopedia Mythica*. Online: http://www.pantheon.org/articles/tiamat.html.

"Universe." NASA. Online: http://www.nasa.gov.

Chapter 7: The Relational God & Chapter 8: Molech

"Shakespeare's Plays." Online: http://www.bardweb.net.

Chapter 13: Woe

http://www.ers.usda.gov/StateFacts

http://www.winespectator.com

http://www.wineinstitute.org ("Statistics")

Chapter 16: Seeing God

Online: http://www.charlierose.com, "A conversation with Dr. Stephen Hawking and Lucy Hawking," 2008; and "A conversation with Martin Rees," 2008. Online: http://www.pbs.org/moyers/faithandreason – an interview with Sir John Houghton, July, 2006.

Chapter 19: Existential Threat

Online: http://www.royal.gov.uk/HistoryoftheMonarchy.

Chapter 21: Gloom and Deliverance

http://www.gfhandel.org

http://www.tks.org/HANDEL/Messiah.htm

http://www.christianitytoday.com/global/printer.htme?/history/special/131christians/handel

Chapter 25: Trees, Beasts, and Peace

http://www.eutopia.no/ymirsbody.html

Chapter 27: Globalization

http://www.cia.gov.library/publications/the-world-factbook
http://australia.gov.au/about-australia/australian-stories/history-colonial
www.news.bbc.co.uk/2/hi/country_profiles

Chapter 30: Meaning

Online: http://www.bbc.co.uk./cult/hitchhikers/guide

Chapter 33: Zen Prophecy

http://www.dharma-rain.org